Man vs. God

GAINING THE WORLD AND LOSING YOUR SOUL

Jerry Hensley

TRILOGY CHRISTIAN PUBLISHERS
TUSTIN, CA

Trilogy Christian Publishers
A Wholly Owned Subsidiary of Trinity Broadcasting Network
2442 Michelle Drive
Tustin, CA 92780

Man vs. God

Copyright © 2022 by Jerry Hensley

Trilogy Christian Publishers
A Wholly Owned Subsidiary of Trinity Broadcasting Network
2442 Michelle Drive Tustin, CA 92780

No part of this book may be reproduced, stored in a retrieval system, or transmitted by any means without written permission from the author. All rights reserved. Printed in the USA.

Rights Department, 2442 Michelle Drive, Tustin, CA 92780.

Trilogy Christian Publishing/TBN and colophon are trademarks of Trinity Broadcasting Network.

Cover design by Jeff Summers

For information about special discounts for bulk purchases, please contact Trilogy Christian Publishing.

Trilogy Disclaimer: The views and content expressed in this book are those of the author and may not necessarily reflect the views and doctrine of Trilogy Christian Publishing or the Trinity Broadcasting Network.

Manufactured in the United States of America

10 9 8 7 6 5 4 3 2 1

Library of Congress Cataloging-in-Publication Data is available.

ISBN: 978-1-68556-378-3

E-ISBN: 978-1-68556-379-0

Dedication

I have been blessed to be part of some amazing people's lives. This book is dedicated to:

My Papaw, Albert Davis. My love of history came from you.

My dad, Bob Hensley. You taught me to stand up for what I knew was right.

My friend and brother, Phil Mashburn. We solved the world's problems many times.

My son, Zac Hensley. Stay on the path you're on. You are incredible.

My wife, Nancy Hensley. You are a Proverbs 31 wife and a daily blessing.

Contents

Introduction vii
Prologue... ix
Chapter One. The 1900s 1
Chapter Two. The 1910s.. 11
Chapter Three. The 1920s 30
Chapter Four. The 1930s 39
Chapter Five. The 1940s 47
Chapter Six. The 1950s.. 60
Chapter Seven. The 1960s 69
Chapter Eight. The 1970s................................... 82
Chapter Nine. The 1980s 90
Chapter Ten. The 1990s 100
Chapter Eleven. The 2000s 116
Chapter Twelve. The 2010s 128
Chapter Thirteen. The 2020s 137
Epilogue... 142
Endnotes 145

Introduction

I've had many people tell me that they didn't discuss politics or religion. After hearing this, these are people I generally avoid. If you dismiss the two events that drive your life, the only other topics are "weather" types. The reason people will not discuss those two topics is that the art of debate and discussion has been lost. If you take an opposing viewpoint, you're wrong, and an argument ensues.

This book illustrates how over a short twelve decades, God's church has suffered as we have chosen to follow our sinful nature. This is one of the reasons we can no longer discuss ideas and alternative viewpoints. Our sinful nature has convinced us that we are powerful and we are right. While we know this idea is absurd, we avoid supposed difficult topics to highlight our foolishness.

Politics and religion should be debated, discussed, and dissected. God wants us to study His Word. How can we study in any real sense if we keep all of our thoughts and questions to ourselves?

In the past, we went to war for our beliefs. Now we are civilized and are not sure what we believe.

Read, discuss, argue if necessary. But at least be sure you understand what you believe.

Prologue

> *There is no neutral ground in the universe. Every square inch, every split second is claimed by God and counterclaimed by Satan.*[1]
>
> —C. S. Lewis

Since the Book of Genesis, man has attempted to show they are not only equals with God but superior. It started in the Garden of Eden when first Eve and then Adam decided to eat the forbidden fruit. You could argue it was the Serpent that fooled them; however, God gave us free will, so they could have chosen to obey God. Just as he always does, Satan knew that by saying, "For God knows that when you eat from it your eyes will be opened, and you will be like God, knowing good and evil" (Genesis 3:5, NIV). It was the "being like God" that caused the Fall because in the next verse,

> When the woman saw that the fruit of the tree was good for food and pleasing to the

eye, and also desirable for gaining wisdom, she took some and ate it. She also gave some to her husband, who was with her, and he ate it. Then the eyes of both of them were opened, and they realized they were naked; so they sewed fig leaves together and made coverings for themselves.

Genesis 3:6–7 (NIV)

It would be this idea, this "wanting to be like God" that continues to drive humanity.

Christian author and apologist C. S. Lewis would write: "The essential vice, the utmost evil, is Pride."[2] It is from pride that all other sins arise from. With that original want of wishing to be like God, man would go one and try to instill himself at the leader in every situation.

At the beginning of the 20th century, roughly 90 percent of adults attended church at least once a week. Most of them attended several times a week. Today, only 56 percent of millennials profess a religious belief. If you look at the time as a whole, one century is just one minuscule part of it. So, what was it about the 20th century that brought about such a change?

It would happen partly because the 20th century would see a hundred years of war. However, that would not be enough. The old adage of "There are no atheists in foxholes" would be proven because, by the end of both world wars, there would be revivals.

The western world's founding documents are based, at least in part, on Scripture and the laws therein. This was done because 90 percent, possibly more, of the population were believers. It was because of this foundation, this foundational belief, that the western world has been able to survive and even thrive.

Since 1900, there has been a very defined shift away from Christianity. This has occurred for several reasons. One of the reasons is that today "nearly four-in-ten (39 percent) report that they are in religiously mixed marriages, compared with 19 percent among those who got married before 1960."[3] This is despite the fact that we were warned about this. In the Book of Judges, we read that

> The Israelites lived among the Canaanites, Hittites, Amorites, Perizzites, Hivites and Jebusites. They took their daughters in marriage and gave their own daughters to their sons, and served their gods. The Israelites did evil in the eyes of the LORD; they forgot the LORD their God and served the Baals and the Asherahs.
>
> Judges 3:5–7 (NIV)

We are to spread the Good News; unfortunately, one of the ways we have chosen to do that is to live among them and marry. Satan has convinced us that if we marry nonbelievers, we can convert them. King Solomon, one of the wisest men who ever lived, made the same mistake. He wasn't smart enough to see what would happen, even though he knew the Scripture. Why do we think we're smarter than Solomon?

Over the last 120 years, there has been a very defined shift away from Christianity. The following book will try to show how, through our prideful nature, we have fought God on every level and on every subject. When that happens, there is only one outcome.

The 1890s would see what was called New Imperialism. This was characterized by a period of colonial expansion by the United States, Russia, and Japan. Each of these countries began to focus on territorial acquisitions. This would include almost all of Africa and parts of Asia.

The end of the 19th century would see the Klondike Gold Rush between 1896 and 1899; roughly 100,000 prospectors would find their way to the Yukon, in north-western Canada. Because it was such a long journey for most of them, and because most of them were so unsuccessful, it became necessary for the Canadian authorities to require each of them to bring a year's supply of food. The equipment weighed close to a ton, which most carried themselves in stages.

In the United Kingdom, George Williams would found the Young Men's Christian Association (YMCA). George Williams was born in October 1821 in Dulverton, Somerset, England. Although he came from a family of farmers, he would become an apprentice at Hitchcock & Rogers, a fabric shop in London. In 1844, he was promoted to department manager.

Williams had long ago become a believer and proselyted at his shop. However, with his promotion, he also believed that "from everyone who has been given much, much will be demanded; and from the one who has been entrusted with much, much more will be asked."[4] This was also the year he and eleven others would start the Young Men Christian's Association. With this, the YMCA was born. They were concerned about the lack of healthy activities for young men in major cities. At the time, the options available were usually taverns and brothels. He wanted a place for fellowship, where men would discover "muscular Christianity." Williams would say that "our object is the improvement of the spiritual condition of the young men engaged in houses of business, by the formation of Bible classes, family and social prayer meetings, mutual improvement societies, or any other spiritual agency." The YMCA would quickly have branches throughout Europe and by the late 19th century would also be in the United States. Churches would see a boom in the 1880s and 1890s. The United States would see the highest levels yet known in the history of the nation. It could be said, though, that even by the 1880s, liberal voices were working within the churches to soften the message, to, even then, make it more inclusive. However, this was also the end of the Second Great Awakening, a period of spiritual growth across Europe and the United States. One of the things that would occur because of the Awakening was the founding of the Salvation Army. It was founded by William and Katherine Booth.

William Booth was born in Nottingham, United Kingdom, in 1829. By the time he was thirteen, his family's finances were so dismal that he would be apprenticed to a pawnbroker. Two years later, he would become a believer, whereas his only goal for the rest of his life seemed to be to spread the Good News. In 1848, his apprenticeship over, he became a lay minister. However, by 1852, he would give up the pawnbroker job and go into ministry full time. He would marry Catherine Mumford in 1855. Even at a young age, she would spend time in the Word, and it was said that she had gone through the entire Bible eight times before the age of twelve.

Through the crowds they began ministering to, they began working with a group of Christian businessmen who were concerned for the poor and disadvantaged in their community. In June 1865, Booth preached to crowds outside the Blind Beggar pub. Shortly thereafter, a new organization, The Christian Mission, was born. The Christian Mission would be the initial name of the Salvation Army and would keep that title until 1878. He replaced "volunteer" with "salvation" and re-christened the organization. They say their mission is "bringing people to understand God."[5] This is done in ways big and small. Over the ensuing 150 years, they had ministered, clothed, and housed hundreds of thousands of individuals.

Motion pictures would see their formation in the latter part of the 19th century. Building on previous inventions, in 1888 in New York City, Thomas Edison and his British assistant, William Dickson, created a device that could record moving pictures. By 1890, "Dickson unveiled the Kinetograph, a primitive motion picture camera. In 1892 he announced the invention of the Kinetoscope, a machine that could project the moving images onto a screen."[6] By the end of the 19th century, the battle had begun; the battle of choosing the secular over the heavenly, as much as individuals knew Scripture and were aware of the warning in Matthew that "For where your treasure is, there your heart will be also" (Matthew 6:21, NIV). If seen in that light, most will make the obvious choice. However, the problem became that more and more believers were becoming fooled, for lack of a better word.

The following chapters will demonstrate how, decade after decade, people began to believe differently despite what Scripture taught. They began to believe, among other things. They believed that living together instead of getting married was okay. They began to put their trust in man. They would begin to open their shops and businesses on the Sabbath. In each category, we began to fight God for control.

As we've won, we've lost.

CHAPTER ONE

The 1900s

Nineteen hundred would see the Exposition Universelle of 1900, known in English as the 1900 Paris Exposition. This World's Fair was held in Paris, France, from April 14 to November 12, 1900. The goal was to celebrate the achievements of the past century and to accelerate development into the next. It would be visited by nearly 50 million. Some of the innovations were the Ferris Wheel, the moving sidewalk, diesel engines, talking films, escalators, and something called the "telegraphone" (the first magnetic audio recorder).

Along with the above-mentioned inventions, two more that are still with us today are the airplane and the automobile. Two bicycle builders from Ohio, Orville and Wilbur Wright, would successfully figure out powered flight, although the first flight would be just a few seconds.

The auto had been around in some form for a couple of decades, but Henry Ford would create the assembly line, and thus the Model T, created by the Ford Motor

Company in 1908, would become the first automobile to be mass-produced on a moving assembly line.

Henry Adams, the grandson of President John Quincy Adams and great-grandson of President John Adams, saw the coming onslaught of technology. He also saw how it would affect us. He predicted the war that would arise. He referred to it as the "the Dynamo" vs. the Virgin. Technology was the Dynamo that would, if allowed to, sweep away "the essential undergirdings of humanity—religion and traditional values—which he christens the Virgin."[7] Adams would predict that "science will be the master of man. The engines he will have invented will be beyond his strength to control. Someday, science shall have the existence of mankind in its power, and the human race (will) commit suicide by blowing up the world."[8] Due to his ancestors' inability to place politics over the truth, neither John nor John Quincy would be elected to a second term. Henry Adams would suffer much the same fate and be ridiculed during his lifetime for much of what he said. It would only be later his words would be taken seriously.

God would give us the knowledge to create, and we have done that. Some have been labor-saving devices and would be beneficial. Technology would soon invade the life of everyone, believer and non-believer alike. We would find many ways to add technology to everything from automobiles to refrigerators. As this was done, our dependence was placed more and more on things and less and less on Him.

By 1900, the United States had established itself as a world power after the end of the Spanish-American War. As a result of this, they had acquired Guam, Puerto Rico, and a large part of the Philippines. The country that had once been satisfied to simply manage itself now began to combine its resources with other western countries.

Many of President William McKinley's opponents would argue that the land acquired by the United States was the beginning of the American president building colonies, with his eye on world domination. In truth, McKinley's eye was on another world. A heavenly one. In reality, McKinley had wanted the islands because it was his goal to "educate the Filipinos, and uplift and civilize and Christianize them and by God's grace do the very best we could by them, as our fellow men for whom Christ also died."[9] McKinley was one of the last American presidents to have a strong Christian faith and was not ashamed to talk about it.

McKinley was born on January 29, 1843, in Niles, Ohio. He would join the Methodist Church at sixteen and would seek God's guidance for the rest of his life. After his service with the Union Army was complete, he studied law, opened an office in Canton, Ohio, and would eventually enter politics. His wife, Ida, suffered from a myriad of debilitating diseases, including epilepsy, and was almost an invalid by the time he ran for the presidency. He placed his wife above his career and ran what was called a "front porch campaign." McKinley never left her side and gave speeches to crowds gathered around his front porch.

Placing his covenant with both God and his wife above any earthly gains would be something unheard of from many politicians since then.

God and the Workplace

My share of the work may be limited, but the fact that it is work makes it precious.[10]

—Helen Keller

The Industrial Revolution would change the world very quickly. It would begin roughly around 1760 and end in 1840. Those eight decades would see machines replace many hand production methods, new chemical manufacturing and iron production processes, and the rise of the mechanized factory system. It led to important developments in transportation and communication, including the steam locomotive, steamship, telegraph, and radio.

It began in Great Britain but then moved to Belgium and eventually worked its way into France and the United States. The mechanization of labor made factories increasingly tedious and sometimes dangerous. These changes "would fuel the formation of labor unions, as well as the passage of new child labor laws and public health regulations in both Britain and the United States."[11] The improvements that were made are still impacting us today.

Most of the world's population were farmers before this began. Because factories could increase production, more manpower was needed. This began the move from rural to urban communities. The inventions that would be created in the next one hundred years would have their roots in the Revolution. These labor-saving devices would give us more free time. Some of the earliest would include a mechanical sewing machine with a "1755 British patent issued to German, Charles Weisenthal,"[12] the dishwasher in 1850, and electric mixers in 1858. However, the adage of "Idle hands are the devil's workshop" would prove to be true.

The expansion of a workforce meant that each country would have more wealth, which would lead to a rush for more material possessions. This would, in many ways, lead to the thirst for wealth from both governments, churches, and men.

In the guise of needing revenue to finance the Civil War, the United States government passed the Revenue Act of 1861, which "levied, collected, and paid, upon the annual income of every person residing in the United States, whether such income is derived from any kind of property, or from any profession, trade, employment, or vocation carried on in the United States or elsewhere, or from any other source whatever."[13] This Act was supposed to only finance the war and then disappear. But the United States government would find a way, as would every other government, to continue the cash flow.

Prayers in the Workplace

If you search successful business organizations, you will see the most successful have combined their Christian beliefs into their secular pursuits. One such example is John D. Rockefeller, the founder of Standard Oil Company.

The Standard Oil Company originated in 1863, and by 1880, it controlled around 95 percent of *all* the refined oil in the United States. President Theodore Roosevelt would go after the company during his administration for being a monopoly; however, it was the success of Standard Oil that allowed his Christian nature to be shown.

Rockefeller's mother Eliza had infused her son with her Baptist teachings, those of hard work, tithing, and philanthropy. He would say that "charity is injurious unless it helps the recipient to become independent of it."[14] While many of both his contemporaries and future historians would deride Rockefeller, by the end of his life "in total, historians estimate that he gave away $550,000,000 (almost $1 billion in 21st-century dollars), which is more than any other American before him."[15] This meant that he would, at least in part, show businesses how to be both successful and a philanthropist.

God's Idea of Work

Scripture is full of examples of what God thinks of mankind's work ethic. One of the earliest is after the Fall, when man is cursed, "By the sweat of your brow you will eat your food until you return to the ground, since from it you were taken; for dust you are and to dust you will return" (Genesis 3:19, NIV). One of the three consequences of our disobedience was that we were to earn our living. Mankind found a way to override God's command.

Man's Idea of Work

One of the results of the social construct that would begin with the expansion of labor would be both governments and individuals would begin to find ways of getting paid without a physical labor. As a result of this growth, man began to believe they were responsible for their economic success. On one side of this were the employers, the ones who had built their companies. Those companies would begin to sell stock. Those stockholders would begin to control more and more of the economy. This speculative process, betting that stock you will buy will be worth more in the future. These gamblers would cause many of the world's problems by putting so much of their time chasing earthly treasure. One example of this would be the stock market crash of 1929 which would cause the Great Depression.

On the other side, the workers would form alliances, termed "unions." One of the earliest was the Industrial Workers of the World (IWW). The IWW was founded in Chicago in 1905 and is open to membership from "students, retirees, the unemployed, the self-employed, those in informal professions, and those unable to work may also join...the IWW is One Big Union."[16] Another program that would weaken God's idea of work was Unemployment Insurance.

The United Kingdom would enact two social insurance laws in 1911. They would be "an unemployment insurance law which pays the worker weekly benefits with his unemployment results from lack of work, and the other a health insurance law providing medical services, and cash benefits when he is unable to work because of sickness."[17] The idea of getting paid for working was not

God's plan. The reason this idea was accepted initially was the disparity of the Depression. As economic times improved, however, individuals and families found they relied upon the money and were not willing to follow God's plan and work. They chose to follow man and began to find ways to scam the system.

This would ensure that political leaders, regardless of a party, would begin to exploit the idea of money for quote quid pro quo; thus, more people would chase the government instead of God.

By the end of the century's first decade, President McKinley would be the third American president assassinated in forty years. McKinley would be the last American president to openly talk about God until Jerry Ford in the 1970s. His immediate successors, Teddy Roosevelt and Woodrow Wilson, would put their faith in the state, not God.

The 1900s would be the last decade when there would not be a considerable number of women in the workplace. This would occur in the 1910s and the 1940s because of world wars and in the 1930s because of the need for extra income per the Depression. However, the changing world of the 1950s, the growing social awareness of wives to "have it all," the growing tax burdens, and the laxing morals of the 1960s and 1970s would cause the family to weaken.

Women would be told they didn't "need a man." The family began to break down, the husband or wife would be replaced by a live-in boyfriend or girlfriend. As the family eroded, the church could have found ways to strengthen it. But they were falling victim to the same morass that was affecting every other area of life.

CHAPTER TWO

The 1910s

The second decade of the century would see the formation of many things. One would be motion pictures. Some of the earliest movies were historical, as there were movies about Abraham Lincoln. Some were early versions of Frankenstein and the Wizard of Oz. However, it would also include the first porno.

Called *Am Abend* ("In the Evening"), this ten-minute long German film would become one of the first hardcore pornographic movies. Although the bulk of movies before the 1960s would be of the more conservative type, the pornos would come into the mainstream and become "respectable."

Another movie that would change society for the worse would be *Birth of a Nation*, the 1915 film that depicted blacks in an extremely negative light and was pro Ku Klux Klan (KKK). After the film hit theaters, the KKK, which had been waning in both popularity and membership, began to swell its ranks. It would go on to become the first movie shown at the White House to the overtly-racist President Woodrow Wilson. He would go on to espouse the greatness of the film.

One of the biggest organizations that would have its roots at the end of 1900 and the beginning of 1910 was the Boy Scout Organization. It was created by Lieutenant General Robert Stephenson Smyth Baden-Powell, 1st Baron Baden-Powell. Powell was born in February 1857 and would be a British Army officer, serving as a soldier from 1876 until 1910.

He would write the first editions of *Scouting for Boys*. His sister Agnes would, at the same time, create the Girl Scouts. He seems to be a firm believer in the adage of "idle hands are the devil's workshop." Baden-Powell would write in the first *Scouting for Boys* that,

> There is a vast reserve of loyal patriotism and Christian spirit lying dormant in our nation today, mainly because it sees no direct opportunity for expressing itself...there is vast opportunity open to all in a happy work that shows results under your hands and a work that is worthwhile because it gives every man his chance of service for his fellow-men and for God.[18]

By 1910, the Scouting organization had found its way to the United States. Since its inception in 1910, "more than 35 million adult volunteers have helped carry out the BSA's mission."[19] Those thirty million have gone on to become writers, ministers, world leaders. They have influenced every part of society and have gone on to impact the lives of the generations that followed.

One of the biggest news stories of that period was the sinking of the RMS Titanic.

The ship would have its beginnings in 1908 when the drawings for the ship were approved by White Star Line. The company was not new to the business as the Titanic was the 400th one it would do. It would be one of the largest ever built at 882 feet 9 inches long with a maximum breadth of 92 feet 6 inches. Her total height, measured from the base of the keel to the top of the bridge, was 104 feet. The ship would be powerful as she was equipped with three main engines—two reciprocating four-cylinder, steam engines with a combined output of 30,000 horsepower as well as one low-pressure Parsons turbine, which added an additional 16,000 horsepower.

The safety features of the Titanic included eleven vertically closing watertight doors that could seal off the compartments in the event of an emergency. With all of the combined power and the safety features, the White Star Line would declare that "not even God himself could sink this ship."[20] God was up for the challenge. It would set sail on April 10, 1912, and would sink on

April 15th after hitting an iceberg. Of the 2,224 passengers and crew aboard, more than 1,500 died.

Due in part to countries beginning to put more confidence in themselves than God, the term militarism came into being. It means that a government should maintain a strong military capability to expand national interests and/or values. In other words, instead of spreading the Good News, they were spreading tales of their own greatness. However, nothing would change the world so quickly as the assassination of Archduke Franz Ferdinand on June 28, 1914.

This would lead to the start of World War I on August 1. The war was called the Great War and The War to End All War; neither title would be accurate. The murder triggered a chain of events and would create alliances. The countries of Germany, Austria-Hungary, and Italy joined forces, the latter having joined when they feared a combined force between the other two would be unstoppable.

The allies would be Great Britain, France, Russia, and eventually, the United States. The leader of the allies, specifically American President Woodrow Wilson, would use the victory in 1918 as an excuse to attempt to control the ideas of war and peace.

One of the lasting changes to the United States would happen in 1913, the creation of the Federal Reserve.

The economy of America before President Woodrow Wilson created the Federal Reserve was similar to the way the Bank of the United States (BUS) operated. The first Bank of the United States was created by the first Secretary of the Treasury, thirty-two-year-old Alexander Hamilton. Hamilton was born out of wedlock in the West Indies and, maybe because of this, seemed to always have a chip on his shoulder and something to prove. He was an influential attorney and, along with James Madison and John Jay, wrote The Federalist Papers, urging support for the new Constitution. As Treasury Secretary, Hamilton designed an entirely new financial system.

However, it would prove a challenge for him. He proposed the government assume the entire debt of the federal government and the states. His plan was to pay off the old loans by borrowing money at lower rates, which would thus serve as operating capital. But states that had already paid off their debts, Maryland, Pennsylvania, North Carolina, and Virginia, saw no reason why they should be taxed, in essence, twice to pay off the debts of the less frugal states.

The bank collected taxes, made loans, and, more importantly, made the financial system truly united. The national bank created a national currency and, by tying together each of the states, gave the national union more borrowing power because they were seen as a good credit risk from abroad.

The bank's charter had been signed into creation originally by George Washington himself.

Critics of the first bank included, among others, future presidents Thomas Jefferson and James Madison. Those critics adopted a position known as strict constructionism. They charged a national bank was unconstitutional since the Constitution did not specifically give Congress the power to create a bank.

It was probably only because it was Hamilton's idea and Washington saw Hamilton as almost a son that Washington signed it into law.

The BUS set the rules for the state banks as far as repaying the loans—one of which was that they must be repaid by specie—or coin money. This was a sticking point with many of them. The state banks wanted more control of the currency, and non-specie paper allowed them to have that. With the expiration of the charter in 1811, control went back to the states.

In 1816, when the second Bank of the United States was being debated in Congress, one of the biggest supporters was Speaker of the House, Henry Clay. Clay had been in politics for over a decade and had been an attorney for ten years before. Clay was one of those figures who was both loved and hated. As an attorney, he had displayed his verbal prowess.

One example of this is one of the cases he was handling. He accidentally argued the evidence the prosecution had against his client. When his client finally got his attention to inform him of the fact, he redirected his argument by saying, "If I was the prosecutor in this case, that is surely what I would be saying; however, I have an argument for each of those points."[21] Clay then went on to refute the evidence he had just argued for and won the case. He would take this ability into the political arena.

However, Clay was in favor of the bank's recharter as he had come to return from to the United States from Belgium. Upon returning to his beloved home in Kentucky, he was able to compare the good of a national bank versus state banks. For the first time, he saw how the larger national scene had been affected.

The charter would again expire after twenty years. Again, Henry Clay was one of the supporters of it and talked about his support in 1832 on his run for the presidency. However, his opponent for both the presidency and the National Bank was Andrew Jackson.

Jackson had first been elected in 1828. He had been a Major General of the United States Army since 1814, after the retirement of William Henry Harrison. He had fought Indians, first the Creek, then the Shawnee, the Seminole, and the Cherokee. He had won treaties, most notably the Treaty of Horseshoe Bend, and he had been victorious at the Battle of New Orleans. Jackson wanted to be viewed as a god, and Clay wouldn't play that game. Therefore, anything Clay was for Jackson was against. Jackson won reelection; the bank did not receive a recharter.

The fact that Jackson had no alternative did not bother him. He had defeated Henry Clay and killed both the rechartering and the BUS. That was all he cared about.

With the death of the BUS came an increase in land speculation. The speculators had deep pockets and, just like the oil speculators a century and a half later, caused inflated prices. The General's solution was the Specie Circular, which Treasury Secretary Levi Woodbury released on July 11, 1836, and said that "after the 15th day of August next, to receive in payment of the public lands nothing except what is directed by the existing laws, viz.: gold and silver."[22] When this happened, the banks recalled most of the paper money and were slow to make loans to the smaller banks, which began the panic of 1837.

The panic of 1837 can be blamed on Jackson. It would last well into 1840, and no politician running for the presidency in the next three decades would have the intestinal fortitude to suggest Jackson was wrong.

God and Politics

> *Bad men cannot make good citizens. It is when people forget God that tyrants forge their chains.*[23]
> —Patrick Henry

Many believers and nonbelievers alike believe that politics and the church don't mix. God and politics work hand-in-hand. Politics does not simply mean how you vote or what you post on social media; politics is a belief system. We are told,

> You are the salt of the earth. But if the salt loses its saltiness, how can it be made salty again? It is no longer good for anything, except to be thrown out and trampled underfoot. You are the light of the world. A town built on a hill cannot be hidden. Neither do people light a lamp and put it under a bowl. Instead they put it on its stand, and it gives light to everyone in the house. In the same way, let your light shine before others, that they may see your good deeds and glorify your Father in heaven.
> Matthew 5:13–16 (NIV)

The only way we are able to be the "Salt and Light" is by living out our lives through normal everyday interactions. By doing so, we are a part of the political systems in our local churches, our jobs, our friends, and our families.

If you study the Bible with more than just a passing read, you will see that believers are commanded to:

> Let everyone be subject to the governing authorities, for there is no authority except that which God has established. The authorities that exist have been established by God. Consequently, whoever rebels against the authority is rebelling against what God has instituted, and those who do so will bring judgment on themselves. For rulers hold no terror for those who do right, but for those who do wrong. Do you want to be free from fear of the one in authority? Then do what is right and you will be commended.
>
> Romans 13:1–3 (NIV)

We are to respect and obey our leaders; however, we must ask, are the leaders following God?

Prayers for Political Leaders

Throughout the Bible, there are prayers both that we are to pray for our leaders and that leaders should pray. Whether we are leaders or not, we are told, "That petitions, prayers, intercession and thanksgiving be made for all people—for kings and all those in authority, that we may live peaceful and quiet lives in all godliness and holiness" (1 Timothy 2:1–2, NIV). In order for this to happen, "Therefore I want the men everywhere to pray, lifting up holy hands without anger or disputing" (1 Timothy 2:8, NIV). The head of the family, or the head of state, is viewed in the same biblically political terms.

That is the problem. In Matthew, we are told, "For where your treasure is, there your heart will be also" (Matthew 6:21, NIV). Therefore, whatever we value as treasure is what we will pursue with passion. For much of the world's history, civilization has been governed by laws that were based on either the Ten Commandments or other Scripture. When that civilization turns its back on God, it gets wiped completely off the face of the earth.

You could look at the cities of Sodom and Gomorrah, or if you want an example to use for a nonbeliever, you could use the Roman Empire.

The Roman Empire was founded when Augustus Caesar proclaimed himself the first emperor of Rome in

31 BC and came to an end about 476 AD. Although that is a relatively long time from mankind's perspective, the Roman fall, as a civilization, came about because of "the punishment (the Emperors) inflicted on the Christians, a sect of men who had embraced a new and criminal superstition."[24] The Roman Empire was, arguably, one of the mightiest empires ever on earth, as large as 5 million square kilometers. However, once they began their descent following the wrong "treasure," their empire would be history.

Just as in every other instance, Scripture includes many examples of praying for our leaders. In Psalms, we read, "The King is mighty, he loves justice—you have established equity; in Jacob, you have done what is just and right" (Psalm 99:4, NIV). It's when we forget which King to pray to that we get in trouble.

God's Idea of Politics

God always meant for us to have mortal rulers and be subservient to God in all of his rulings. The first example of this was in Exodus with Moses. It says, "The next day Moses took his seat to serve as judge for the people, and they stood around him from morning till evening" (Exodus 18:13, NIV). Moses would be one of Israel's first leaders and would guide them through their forty-year trek through the desert and would faithfully, with one exception, follow God. It wasn't until God's people almost demanded a ruler that things began to run out of control. It would be the rulers chosen by God, Moses, and Joshua that would chart the course for both Israel and all believers. One of Joshua's final recorded words to Israel and believers, in general, would be prophetic.

> Joshua said to the people, 'You are not able to serve the LORD. He is a holy God; he is a jealous God. He will not forgive your rebellion and your sins. If you forsake the LORD and serve foreign gods, he will turn and bring disaster on you and make an end of you, after he has been good to you.'
> Joshua 24:19–20 (NIV)

People who proclaim to be Christians would prove time and again this to be true.

Jesus would show a very deliberate division when He said, "Give back to Caesar what is Caesar's and to God what is God's" (Mark 12:17, NIV). The Apostle Paul would say later to Timothy, "For all who rely on the works of the law are under a curse, as it is written: 'Cursed is everyone who does not continue to do everything written in the Book of the Law'" (Galatians 3:10, NIV). Clearly, no one who relies on the law is justified before God because "the righteous will live by faith." However, we have forgotten the dictates of God's laws, and we are being deceptively drawn into believing that many of the organized churches are following God's laws.

Although Satan has always strived to find ways to weaken the faith of believers, however, starting in the 19th century, Satan would have help from believers. The reason that the Pilgrims left England in 1620 was because of religious freedom. The Church of England, under the rule of the Monarch, had passed the Acts of Uniformity laws in 1552 and then expanded them in 1559. The Acts "required all persons to attend worship on Sunday, the latter (the 1559 expansion) imposing a fine for neglect to do so."[25] The Pilgrims, who preferred the name "Saints," would leave, and the result would be a number of revivals or awakenings. The first awakening lasted roughly a decade, with the second covering almost forty. These events would begin revivals that are still spreading the Good News today. However, the problem was free will.

God did not want us as mindless robots but as people who chose to love Him. He would say,

> This day I call the heavens and the earth as witnesses against you that I have set before you life and death, blessings and curses. Now choose life, so that you and your children may live and that you may love the LORD your

God, listen to his voice, and hold fast to him. For the LORD is your life, and he will give you many years in the land he swore to give to your fathers, Abraham, Isaac and Jacob.

Deuteronomy 30:19–20 (NIV)

The awakenings would, either directly or indirectly, result in many different choices for believers.

Martin Luther wrote his 95 Theses, which proclaimed, "They preach only human doctrines who say that as soon as the money clinks into the money chest, the soul flies out of purgatory."[26] This had occurred because the Pope had begun to guarantee that by paying what he called an "indulgence," the payee would be forgiven of their sins. This would result in a denomination called the Lutherans. Also, there would be six princes who would send a formal letter to the Catholic Church in protest. There would be a denomination that would spring up around them that would be known as Protestants. Followers of John Calvin would become Calvinists. John Wesley and his brother, Charles, would found the Methodists.

These denominations would give believers more choices, but it would be the plethora of choices that would cause the pastors of these congregations to compete for the tithing. This would cause, by the 20th century, the messages from the pulpit to become so watered down as to neither offend nor convict anyone.

Man's Idea of Politics

We, as believers, know that the government of earth is superseded by the government of heaven. This is reinforced because when Jesus first appears in the Bible, John the Baptist exclaims, "The time has come. The kingdom of God has come near. Repent and believe the good news!" (Mark 1:15, NIV). However, over the intervening centuries, we have demanded more and more control. We are told to obey our leaders. However, as believers, we are to hold our leaders accountable.

Woodrow Wilson was born on December 28, 1856, in Staunton, Virginia. Wilson's father, Joseph, was a prominent Presbyterian minister who used the pulpit to promote his racist views that whites were superior to every other race. In his sermon at the First Presbyterian Church on January 6, 1861, he delivers one of his typical messages. He said the word "slave," since it is used in the Bible, is condoned by God. Furthermore,

> The word is never employed to indicate the condition of a mere hireling. It points out a dependent who is solely under the authority of a master: that master being the head of a

household and wielding over his slaves the commission of a despot, whose acts are to be determined only by the restraining laws of Christianity and by general considerations of his own and their welfare: a despot responsible to God, a good conscience, and the well-being of society. I use the word 'despot' advisedly. It is the scriptural opposite of 'slave.'[27]

This idea of white superiority would morph into an idea that he, Woodrow Wilson, knew better. He began to see himself as the master of the United States, and by the end of WWI, the master of the world.

When he campaigned for reelection in 1916, his slogan was "He Kept Us Out Of War." A month after beginning his second term, he would send troops into battle. Wilson's commanding general would say that Wilson must enter the war and keep his troops separate "for his own purpose." His own purpose was to end war completely.

By 1918, with the war winding down, Wilson began championing the League of Nations, which was largely his brainchild. The League was the precursor of the United Nations and was, according to Wilson, the "only power to put behind the liberation of mankind, and that is the power of mankind. It is the power of the united moral forces of the world, and in the covenant of the league of nations the moral forces of the world are mobilized."²⁸ In other words, only man is powerful enough to control the future. This idea was a huge departure from the thinking just a decade earlier. Wilson was so ostracized by the trying to single-handedly create a world government that when it came time for the United States to join, even his fellow Democrats in Congress voted no. Ultimately, since even its stronger supporter wouldn't join, the League only existed until the 1940s.

Even though he had been raised in the church, he understood very little about God, heaven, or anything beyond the earthly realm. He would close the above speech by saying, "We have accepted that truth, and we are going to be led by it, and it is going to lead us, and through us, the world, out into pastures of quietness and peace such as the world never dreamed of before."²⁹ With the world focusing on a World War and the treaty that ended it, much was not focused on an event that would have a much larger impact.

Because of what would become known as the October Revolution in 1917, Vladimir Ilyich Ulyanov would become the first and founding head of the government of Soviet Russia. Ulyanov, known as Lenin, was born in April 1870. He would be the leader of what would become known as Communism. The revolution that would sweep him to power is also known as the Bolshevik Revolution, and many see that as the most significant political event of the 20th century. But it was more than the creating of a party. He and his followers were attempting to overthrow Christianity itself. He would say that "all worship of a divinity is a necrophilia."[30] It can be said that wherever Communism spreads, Christianity wanes. Communism would preach that government was god, the only god. As this idea caught on, many of the teachings of Scriptures would become less important, weakened, laughed at.

One of the results of the October Revolution was the idea of the no-fault divorce. The new no-fault divorce law was enacted that following December. It was done to undermine the institution of marriage itself, and by this invention, it was felt that marriage would be taken from a holy union to a man-made one. Once the idea moved from Russia to other countries, this is exactly what happened. It could be said that in the beginning, God gave us commandments, and man would begin to make them guidelines.

Wilson, as someone brought up in the church, should have been the ideal candidate to show the world why God, and not the state, was Who we need to align ourselves with. Both individually and as a country. Wilson instead took the world stage, and the world saw that his ideals were close to Lenin's. This would reinforce the idea that it was man, and his ideas, that were most important.

CHAPTER THREE

The 1920s

By the beginning of the decade, this idea would be reinforced after Wilson left office. The new American president had campaigned on what the world wanted after the end of the war, a "Return to Normalcy." However, the return that they wanted would not occur. That would be because of one thing: Money. The 1920s would be a time of prosperity. One of the successful slogans politicians ran on during this period was "a chicken in every pot and a car in every backyard."[31] Because of the economic prosperity that occurred, it was called the "Roaring Twenties" in America and the "Golden Twenties" in Europe.

What was typical for the decade, regardless of the continent you were on, was that your nation's total wealth doubled between that ten-year period. One of the biggest benefactors during this decade was Venezuela. The South American country began exporting oil and was soon the largest in the world. The first "consumer society" began, thanks in part to the spread of chain stores and the same advertising throughout the entire country.

This prosperity would continue to draw individuals away from churches. Fashions would change, hemlines would rise. In the United States, prohibition declared alcohol illegal. This meant that a simple vice now became dangerous, and thus, more desirable. The Eighteenth Amendment to the United States Constitution prohibited the "manufacture, sale, or transportation of intoxicating liquors within, the importation thereof into, or the exportation thereof from the United States and all territory subject to the jurisdiction thereof for beverage purposes."[32] Because of this, organized crime, which had arrived in the United States when they were still British colonies, greatly expanded their reach and their finances. They would form alliances with people in every walk of life, public and private. We are still victims of many of those affiliations today.

By the 1920s, most cities had electricity and indoor plumbing. Most of the rural communities still did not. This can be seen as one reason why, according to the United States Census of 1920, more people now lived in cities than did in rural communities.

Due in part to the atrocities seen during the War, but also because of what many saw as their nation in danger of becoming morally bankrupt, many began to pray in earnest for revival. In Europe, this led to a series of revivals in which "12,409 people were counselled in the inquiry rooms; many churches gained additions, some a hundred, some double;...prayer meetings, Bible classes and missionary meetings all increased in strength."[33] The United States would have what many would term a "rural revival." Even though the population surrounding these churches in rural communities was mostly rural, the revival would spread into the cities as well.

Many Christian leaders at the time became convinced that the way to draw people back to church was to secularize Jesus and the Good News. To that end, they rewrote many of the ideas in Scripture. For example, in a book called *The Man Nobody Knows*, author Bruce Barton says that, in essence, Jesus needs better ad-men. He would write that, "If he were to live again, in these modern days, he would find a way to make them [his works] known—to be advertised by his service, not merely his sermons."[34] There are several things wrong with this premise. First, Barton calls Jesus, per the title, a man. Second, he says, "If he were to live again." If the person who is trying to persuade people to return to church thinks Jesus is dead, then he is the last person who should be trying to persuade.

The problem was, though, that people *did* need to hear and re-hear the truth. They *did* need to be turned back to church. But even less than two decades into the new century, those who were trying were turning from the truth while trying to find the truth at the same time.

God and Money

Make money your God, and it will plague you like the devil.[35]

—Henry Fielding

You've heard the adage that says, "Money is the root of all evil." This is one of many adages that are often misquoted. The entire quote says, "For the love of money is a root of all kinds of evil" (1 Timothy 6:10, NIV). Money in itself is not evil; it is just another thing, another commodity. However, the love of money will cause an otherwise sane individual to do what they know to be irrational things. Individuals from every country in the world, from every social structure, will kill, lie, and align themselves with people who will do anything and everything to obtain one more dollar, or euro, or yen or bitcoin. Name a monetary system, and there are people who want more of it.

Prayers to Use with Money

To understand money, as the way used in this context, you must separate the way that God views it and the way the world sees it. Money, whether metal or paper, only has value because someone says it does. It has been part of history for at least the last 3,000 years. Even before a monetary system was in place, bartering was in place. Bartering was the original form of currency that was simply trading "goods or services in exchange for other goods or services."[36] Farmers would trade with carpenters or other tradesmen or with doctors. In this way, everyone had what they needed. Ultimately, societies moved away from the barter system when leaders began to learn that a monetary system was more controllable. Slowly, a type of currency evolved. Sometimes it could be animal skins, salt, weapons, or literally hundreds of other items. This system of trading spread across the world, and it still survives today in some parts of the globe. Slowly, it evolved again until it was precious stones or metals dug out of the earth. As the world continued to become smaller and countries began selling to other countries, what was considered "money" changed again.

The precious metals that every country gave value to slowly gave way to paper currency, again because the market of the paper was more easily adjusted. Today, we have digital money, created to simply give value to something as insignificant as paper itself. These digital "coins" mean that the bit, the meaningless series of ones and zeroes that store data, have the same as the amethyst, diamond, and gold that God created.

This is the system that each of us, believers and nonbelievers alike, struggle against every day. Since we live in the physical world, we must use it as any other tool that God gave us to use. However, we are warned that "For where your treasure is, there your heart will be also" (Matthew 6:21, NIV). Unfortunately for many of us, monetary wealth is the treasure we chase.

What has happened, just as in every other situation, is that we have convinced ourselves that all the wealth we have, we have created ourselves. Moses cautioned us, however, that,

> You may say to yourself, 'My power and the strength of my hands have produced this wealth for me.' But remember the LORD your God, for it is he who gives you the ability to produce wealth, and so confirms his covenant, which he swore to your ancestors, as it is today.
>
> Deuteronomy 8:17–18 (NIV)

Keeping a thankful heart for everything He has blessed us with, including what others count as "wealth," is the key to understanding the role it is to play in your life.

To many, even believers, the word "tithe" is a dirty word. Tithing was created as a way to pay the tribe of Levi. It was this tribe that became responsible for ministering to the other tribes. Since their focus was:

> It is the Levites who are to do the work at the tent of meeting and bear the responsibility for any offenses they commit against it. This is a lasting ordinance for the generations to come. They will receive no inheritance among the Israelites. Instead, I give to the Levites as their inheritance the tithes that the Israelites present as an offering to the LORD. That is why I said concerning them: 'They will have no inheritance among the Israelites.'
> Numbers 18:23–24 (NIV)

So, initially, tithing was done to allow those who ministered to focus completely on God and to pass on His message. This tithe, which means "tenth," has evolved. Now instead of living simply, communing with God, most western civilizations have built megachurches.

God's Idea of Money

The most important thing to remember is that all wealth, like everything else, is God's, not ours. More than anything else that we come in contact with on a daily basis, money dominates us. God tells us the value He places on our ideas of money when He asks, "Why spend money on what is not bread, and your labor on what does not satisfy? Listen, listen to me, and eat what is good, and you will delight in the richest of fare" (Isaiah 55:2, NIV). Wealth has become how we're measured. Wealth, and hence, power, is what we desire, believers and nonbelievers alike.

Man's Idea of Money

Our chase of the dollar is part of our punishment for the Fall. Actually, it's *man's* punishment. After Adam ate the forbidden fruit, he was told, "By the sweat of your brow you will eat your food until you return to the ground" (Genesis 3:19, NIV). Woman was never intended to work outside the home. That happened as a result of policies that increased revenue to the government through an endless procession of taxes and the subtle prodding that single-parent homes are "normal."

There are many experts who argue that "monetary economists begin a revision of their concepts of money, to draw a distinction between the attributes of money and its substance and to give recognition to the mysterious and awesome force of moral integrity in its management."[37] However, the problem is that the economists that are in charge are in bed with those who want to keep us on the financial hamster wheel. This is where the idea of Keynesian Economics comes into play.

Keynesian Economics is named after John Maynard Keynes, a British economist. The idea was put forth in the 1930s and argued that the only way to have a solid economy was total control by the government. In this way, Keynes said, "Deliberate government action could foster full employment. Keynesian economists claim that the government can directly influence the demand for goods and services by altering tax policies and public expenditures."[38] Because of the Depression that swept the west, the people were okay with the idea of handing over total control of their finances. Governments were more than happy to oblige.

After the Depression ended, no one demanded returning to the economic structure the way it was because most of them had become convinced, through repeatedly being told, that government control was best. This was the idea that Joseph Goebbels meant when he said, "If you tell a lie big enough and keep repeating it, people will eventually come to believe it."[39] Goebbels was one of Hitler's closest advisors and one of the biggest supporters of the final solution. Put your faith in the government, and the government becomes your god.

CHAPTER FOUR

The 1930s

The 1930s would begin with a worldwide depression and end with much of the world involved in yet another war. Since the turn of the century, much of the world's economy began to be intertwined. This meant that because of the stock market crash that happened in the United States in October 1929, the entire world would suffer from what would become known as the Great Depression.

As a result of the Depression, America stopped trading with other countries, which would affect their economies as well. Because of the constricted finances of families, women began to leave the home, looking for work. They were desperate to help their husbands. This led Pope Pius XI to give what would be called Quadragesimo Anno (the Fortieth Year). It was written as a continuation of Pope Leo XIII's address forty years earlier.

Both would focus on economic problems facing families. While Pope Pius agreed that families could use the extra income, he argued against the idea because it was "an intolerable abuse, and to be abolished at all cost, for mothers on account of the father's low wage to be forced to engage in gainful occupations outside the home to the neglect of their proper cares and duties, especially the training of children."[40] As would be proven in the following decades, with neither parent focused on the children, the home and thus the foundation of society suffered.

With women joining the workforce, both employers and politicians saw this as a perfect opportunity. Many working women initially were single, and many would quit once they got married. However, as the sexes began to work together more, it came to be a place where married people would meet other married people. This would evolve into how the others' partner "doesn't understand me." Once women left the home and chose other careers, God's design would suffer.

God and Family

Every single area of life is God's, and the job of the Christian with a biblical worldview is to see the world through God's eyes.[41]

—Chuck Colson

Most believers spend more time at work than they do at home. Think about that for a minute. The only thing you have in common with the people you spend most of your life with is that you walk on the same piece of floor. That was not the original intention, but as is the case with everything, man screwed up God's plan. Initially, the family was together.

The concept of family is not new. Originally, the family was together. Merriam Webster defines family as "the basic unit in society traditionally consisting of two parents rearing their children."[42] While this is politically incorrect, this is the correct definition. Today the home with a husband and a wife raising the kids is the exception rather than the rule. A husband and a wife never being married before, and having their kids after they were married, is a rarity.

The basic family structure of husband and wife raising the kids is how the world defines it. However, if thought of as Scripture defines it, it would be God the husband, the church as the wife raising us, the children. Once the secular version of this weakened, it weakened the other. The family was attacked for this reason.

Prayers for the Family

The family was created "In The Beginning." We tend to think of whatever we do at our "office" as our work. We have been conditioned over the last one hundred and fifty years to spend our lives toiling away minute by minute doing an activity that most of us don't enjoy at all. But that is not what God had in mind for us; the Apostle Paul tells us, "Whatever you do, work at it with all your heart, as working for the Lord, not for human masters" (Colossians 3:23, NIV). We, as believers, are working for our Boss, not our boss.

It was the Fall that separated not only the family but man's ideas of work and family. In the Garden of Eden, our only jobs were to take care of the earth and the animals. Adam and Eve's first two sons, Cain and Abel, would be the first two who followed these two professions. Cain worked the soil, Abel tended to the animals. The rivalry between the two sides of our nature can be seen in these brothers. Cain was jealous of Abel; the reason, as far as Cain was concerned, was that God loved Abel more. The problem, however, was pride. Pride caused the initial riff that led to the world's first murder, but it would also cause the splintering of families.

When the Lord was preparing to destroy the earth with a flood, He could have commanded to simply save himself and his wife. However, "The LORD then said to Noah, 'Go into the ark, you and your whole family, because I have found you righteous in this generation'" (Genesis 7:1, NIV). Just as He was telling us in the beginning, God was telling us that families stay together.

God's Idea of Family

We were given a glimpse of how things should be. When God created the Garden of Eden, He was giving us a preview of heaven. Man was there, and besides the small amount of time needed to take care of the animals, we would have basically spent our time with the Savior.

We read in Psalms,

> How good and pleasant it is when God's people live together in unity! It is like precious oil poured on the head, running down on the beard, running down on Aaron's beard, down on the collar of his robe. It is as if the dew of Hermon were falling on Mount Zion. For there the LORD bestows his blessing, even life forevermore.
>
> Psalm 133 (NIV)

This is, of course, not just for blood relatives as most of us would think of them. Since the Blood of Jesus flows through the veins of every believer, we are all blood relatives.

Once we realize that everyone is our family, this should change how we treat them. It's true that families argue. We all hurt those who are closest to us more often than we should. We say things we shouldn't. We do things we shouldn't. The fact that we do these things to family means very little. We do these things because we are humans, and we are fallen creatures.

Scripture tells us how to interact with each other. Whether we are outside of or inside the home, God tells us, "Do not lie to each other, since you have taken off your old self with its practices and have put on the new self, which is being renewed in knowledge in the image of its Creator" (Colossians 3:9–10, NIV). If we're married, "Wives, submit yourselves to your husbands, as is fitting in the Lord" (Colossians 3:18, NIV), and "Husbands, love your wives and do not be harsh with them" (Colossians 3:19, NIV). Whereas children are instructed to "Obey your parents in everything, for this pleases the Lord" (Colossians 3:20, NIV). In these four verses, the Apostle Paul laid out a blueprint for mankind.

It wasn't as if Paul was smarter than anyone else. He worked with his hands; he was a tentmaker, which allowed him to travel very light and share the Good News whether he was in the pulpit or the pasture. He was, however, educated. Paul was a member of the Pharisees.

The Pharisee ("separatist") party emerged largely out of the group of scribes and sages and were considered the most expert and accurate expositors of Jewish law. As a Pharisee, the Apostle Paul knew the Pentateuch very intimately. The Pentateuch is the first five books of the Bible, written by Moses. They understood the law better than most, and last many believers before and since have used it for their benefit. During his mission, he would be beaten, stoned, shipwrecked, imprisoned, yet he saw each of these as an opportunity to share the Good News.

Man's Idea of Family

The 1930s can be seen as the first time where the family began to splinter. While many believed it began in the 1960s, it can be traced back three decades earlier. A number of the programs created during this time would have, either intentionally or not, to separate the family and to show that the state, not your relatives, and certainly not God, will help you.

One of the first was the Civilian Conservation Corps (CCC). This gave men between eighteen and twenty-five the opportunity to help support the family. During the first three months of the program alone, 275,000 enrolled. Other programs followed, many, such as the Unemployment Insurance, were copies of what European countries have. Others were a socialist utopian dream. FDR created the Agricultural Adjustment Administration, which paid farmers not to grow crops. He also created the Public Works Administration (PWA), which, like the CCC, created work, government. This latter added over $3 billion to the debt its first year alone.

There were churches that helped, but as would see during the COVID-19 pandemic eighty years later, the churches would assist but would spend a great deal of time trying to maintain the number of tithes they had lost. The 1930s would not be the first decade that governmental assistance occurred. However, during the century's third decade, even many of the churches began to see the government as the answer to society's problems. Instead of showing how mighty God is, we were slowly being shown how mighty man was. The problem was that many people were listening.

CHAPTER FIVE

The 1940s

After two decades of sliding away from God, there would be a worldwide event that would realign it, another world war. It would begin on September 1, 1939, when Nazi Germany, under Adolf Hitler, invaded Poland. Following this, the United Kingdom and France subsequently declared war on Germany on the 3rd. The United States would not enter until the end of 1941, and this was only after an attack on Pearl Harbor.

Most Americans still wanted to be an isolationist nation. George Washington would give a Farewell Address in the final days of his presidency in which he would say, as far as our dealings with other countries are concerned, that we should "observe good faith and justice towards all nations; cultivate peace and harmony with all…(however) the great rule of conduct for us in regard to foreign nations is in extending our commercial relations, to have with them as little political connection as possible. Hence, therefore, it must be unwise in us to implicate ourselves by artificial ties in the ordinary vicissitudes of her politics, or the ordinary combinations and collisions of her friendships or enmities."⁴³ This idea of avoiding foreign entanglements would be the idea expressed by every American president until Roosevelt and World War II.

Though many would take issue with his socialist policies, he would be able to see the evil of both Hitler and the Nazi Party and steer the country into a place of preparedness. Many of the companies that had been shuddered since the Depression began making military supplies, mainly to assist the United Kingdom, but to make sure the United States would be ready when the Germans came across the ocean. He would also get the first peace-time draft passed, the Selective Service Act, which is still around today.

God and War

> *In times of war, the law falls silent.*⁴⁴
> —Marcus Tullius Cicero

War is almost as old as Creation itself. The Old Testament is full of wars that are fought as God's people fight against God's enemies. This is God's idea of war. God's idea of war says that there is a definite Good and a definite Evil. In God's idea of war, God tells us to totally destroy His enemies. The order to "Now go, attack the

Amalekites and totally destroy all that belongs to them. Do not spare them; put to death men and women, children and infants, cattle and sheep, camels and donkeys" (1 Samuel 15:3, NIV) is one of many and seems pretty straight-forward.

God and Prayers During War

There's an adage that says, "There are no atheists in foxholes," and my experiences with soldiers have backed this up. However, there are prayers that both soldiers and leaders pray during times of war.

One of the earliest examples of both a prayer and a war cry was with a young David when he was to fight Goliath. Everyone else was scared to fight the giant. He is described as being as tall as "six cubits and a span." A cubit is the "length of the forearm from the elbow to the tip of the middle finger and usually equal to about 18 inches,"[45] and a span is "an English unit of length equal to 9 inches."[46] This would mean that Goliath was over nine feet tall. David's physical size and age are unknown, but David knew more than both Goliath and the rest of the Israelites.

He would say to the giant,

> 'You come against me with sword and spear and javelin, but I come against you in the

> name of the LORD Almighty, the God of the armies of Israel, whom you have defied. This day the LORD will deliver you into my hands, and I'll strike you down and cut off your head. This very day I will give the carcasses of the Philistine army to the birds and the wild animals, and the whole world will know that there is a God in Israel. All those gathered here will know that it is not by sword or spear that the LORD saves; for the battle is the LORD's, and he will give all of you into our hands.'
>
> 1 Samuel 17:45–47 (NIV)

As most believers and unbelievers alike know, it was with a simple stone and slingshot that was David's only physical weapon. But David knew he had a spiritual weapon.

There would be many battles waged throughout the Bible, but they would follow a similar pattern; before a battle, God's people would pray. He would answer by saying,

> 'This is what the LORD, the God of Israel, says: Because you have prayed to me concerning Sennacherib king of Assyria, this is the word the LORD has spoken against him...Who is it you have ridiculed and blasphemed? Against

whom have you raised your voice and lifted your eyes in pride? Against the Holy One of Israel! By your messengers you have ridiculed the Lord.'

Isaiah 37:21–24 (NIV)

Each time, when believers prayed before a battle, they would win.

In a lot of ways, the people we read about in the Bible are very similar to the ones today. There were many that worked with their hands, carpenters, farmers, laborers. There are those who were more skilled, such as lawyers and educators. There are also those who are soldiers. This would be the smallest percentage of the population as the idea of what the American Founding Fathers would refer to as a "standing army." This is because, in biblical times, battles were only conducted when God advised the leaders to do so, and then the people would follow behind either the Ark of the Covenant or, as would be the example set in the book of Jacob with the town of Jericho, the musicians would lead the way.

Actually, the idea of a standing army would be more common on the side of God's enemies. Any account of the Old Testament would see the Moabites, Ammonites, Meunites, Edomites, and numerous other armies would fall before the Israelites. The early Israelites would be farmers and hunters, except for the one tribe that were priests. Joshua would create a small army, but it would not be until the Israelites rejected God as their leader and insisted upon a king that a large military presence would begin. King Saul would be the first attempt at believers picking their own leader instead of simply allowing God to be their leader. The result would be the first instance of God's people following a leader who was not following God.

The battle between David and Goliath can be seen as the first example of a modern-day war. The battle itself took place around 1000 BC, but the braggadocio of the opponent and those watching would be seemingly better qualified for battle who are unwilling to fight.

It would be this last, the reluctance of those seemingly better qualified that would be the most important. There are, of course, many reasons why people don't want to fight. However, if God tells you to do something, regardless of what it is, you do it. There have been many commanders who have declared that "God is on our side." However, there are a few that know that it's more important to be on God's side. One of the examples of this is what has since been called the Dunkirk Miracle.

On May 10, 1940, Hitler's Nazi Party had become an unstoppable rolling force. By 1940, they would have steamrolled Poland, Denmark, Norway, Belgium, the Netherlands, Luxembourg, and France. It was in this last that the Miracle occurred. The United States had not yet entered the war, so much of the fighting for the Allies fell to the British Army. Shortly after the battle began, the British Army found itself outmaneuvered and unprepared. The British had their backs to the sea and were hemmed in by enemies. Prime Minister Winston Churchill found himself "preparing to announce to the public an unprecedented military catastrophe involving the capture or death of a third of a million soldiers."[47] King George VI, who would lead the United Kingdom through one of the most traumatic periods of the 20th century, from December 1936 until his death in 1952, requested that the following Sunday should be observed as a National Day of Prayer. The nation, knowing as many before them that with God all things are possible, devoted itself to prayer in an unprecedented way. There would be hundreds of both eyewitnesses and photographs to confirm overflowing congregations, with long lines outside cathedrals.

Following the day of prayer, Hitler ordered his army to halt, and for three days, the German tanks and soldiers stood idle while an evacuation unfolded. During that time, 800 boats of all sizes and shapes crossed the English Channel to rescue the besieged army. By the time the German Army was finally ordered to renew its attack, over 338,000 troops had been snatched from the beaches, including 140,000 French, Belgian, Dutch, and Polish soldiers. Many of them were to return four years later to liberate Europe. If the Nazis had attacked as planned, the British Isles may have fallen to Germany, and without the United States in the war, the Nazis might have prevailed.

God's Idea of War

The idea of war, as defined by Scripture, is what would be defined in modern-day terms as "no quarter." No quarter is defined as showing "no pity or mercy—used to say that an enemy, opponent, etc., is treated in a very harsh way."[48] With this idea of battle, Scripturally, there must be something we are willing to die for. If everything is thought of Scripturally, it means the battle lines are drawn. That becomes a problem when the line between right and wrong, good and evil, is blurred. It then becomes hard to define something worth dying for.

We first see how God predicts how His people will face adversity when He directed the Israelites to take a longer route because "If they face war, they might change their minds and return to Egypt" (Exodus 13:17, NIV). This was just after they had left the Pharaoh after being enslaved for four hundred years. Even after being a prisoner for ten generations, God knew that with the first sign of adversity, believers would want to give up their freedom. This would happen again and again throughout history; believers and nonbelievers alike were willing to accept a loss of freedom for a perceived security. This has been part of the punishment of the Fall. One of the earliest examples of this is when we are told that "If you fully obey the LORD your God and carefully follow all his commands I give you today, the LORD your God will set you high above all the nations on earth" (Deuteronomy 28:1, NIV). However, the Israelites would make it clear, as do many believers today, that we should be able to make our own decisions, remain completely safe, and suffer no consequences if our choices take us away from God. Man's idea of war is one example of that.

God tells us to when we go to war, be sure He is the first to enter so that,

> When you are about to go into battle, the priest shall come forward and address the army. He shall say: 'Hear, Israel: Today you are going into battle against your enemies. Do not be fainthearted or afraid; do not panic or be terrified by them. For the LORD your God is the one who goes with you to fight for you against your enemies to give you victory.
>
> Deuteronomy 20:2–4 (NIV)

This has a two-fold effect. One is a reminder to us that God is to lead us in all we do; the second is to make sure our enemies know who is leading the battle. By following our own paths, we are making the mistake of believing we are in control, and thus, our results are mixed, at best. This has the side effect of us taking the credit for successful battles and blaming when we lose what we have deemed a "Holy War."

One of the earliest recorded examples of this not in the Bible is the Battle of Tolbiac. The site of the battle was Zülpich, North Rhine-Westphalia, which is about 60 km east of the German-Belgian frontier. It was fought in 496 AD between the Franks against the Alemanni. The Clovis I, who had become King in 491, was of the Arianism doctrine, which proclaimed that "Jesus, as the Son of God, was created by God"[49] and therefore was not eternal.

Although being only sixteen when he became king, he knew how to lead battles successfully. In the years between 491 and the Battle of Tolbiac, he had successfully fought against Syagrius and Soissons. The king's wife, Clotilde, was a Christian and was attempting to convert him. When he began to lose men, he called upon his gods to help them. When the losses multiplied faster, he prayed, "O Jesus Christ, you who as Clotilde tells me are the son of the Living God, you who give succor to those who are in danger, and victory to those accorded who hope in Thee, I seek the glory of devotion with your assistance: If you give me victory over these enemies, and if I experience the miracles that the people committed to your name say they have had, I believe in you, and I will be baptized in your name. Indeed, I invoked my gods, and, as I am experiencing, they failed to help me, which makes me believe that they are endowed with no powers, that they do not come to the aid of those who serve. It's to you I cry now, I want to believe in you if only I may be saved from my opponents."[50] After this, the Alemanni began to run away, their commander was killed, and it quickly ended. He, as well as many of his commanders, would be baptized shortly thereafter.

This is also indicative of a battle fought by God. After it's over, many will see the truth and will want to follow Him.

By the time of Clovis' death in either 511 or 513, depending on which biography you read, he was the ruler over Gaul, which consists of France, Belgium, Luxemburg, and parts of the Netherlands, Switzerland, and Germany on the west bank of the Rhine. He would come to be known as the founder of France, and history would ultimately Latinize his name to Louis, a name that would live on in French royalty for centuries through eighteen kings and remains popular in French culture to the present day.

Man's Idea of War

However, in man's idea of war, mankind has decided over the intervening years to use its free will and use war for its own purposes. War has become the same as everything in the fallen world, another way for us to show our dominance over each other.

However, instead of relying on God's instruction as to how to proceed in war, we have allowed secular war heroes to define our war strategies. Sun Tzu, born in 544 BC, was a Chinese general, military strategist, writer, and philosopher and would write *The Art of War* that would become a playbook for many strategists. He would say, "It is only one who is thoroughly acquainted with the evils of war that can thoroughly understand the profitable way of carrying it on…Thus it may be known that the leader of armies is the arbiter of the people's fate, the man on whom it depends whether the nation shall be in peace or in peril."[51] Even before the time of Christ's birth, mankind had convinced itself that man led the war.

This doesn't mean that evil no longer exists. Evil has been around since Creation, but thanks to the Fall, we have been willing to negotiate with it. One example of this is Prime Minister Neville Chamberlain. He would believe an agreement could be reached in 1938 with Hitler and was determined to prevent a war by any means.

To this end, Hitler met in Munich with Chamberlain, Italian leader Benito Mussolini, and French premier Edouard Daladier to "discuss a diplomatic resolution to the crisis. The four leaders, without any input from Czechoslovakia in the negotiation, agreed to cede the Sudetenland to Hitler. Chamberlain also separately drafted a non-aggression pact between Britain and Germany that Hitler signed."[52] After the agreement, surprise, surprise, he did not honor the agreement.

God tells us to "Be strong and courageous, because you will lead these people to inherit the land I swore to their ancestors to give them" (Joshua 1:6, NIV). Man tells us to fear everything and let the warlords take care of everything.

CHAPTER SIX

The 1950s

The threat of constant war would begin in the middle of the century, which is ironic because, at the end of World War II, the Allies created the United Nations (UN). The purpose of the UN was "to maintain international peace and security, and to that end: to take effective collective measures for the prevention and removal of threats to the peace."[53] In 1938 British Prime Minister Neville Chamberlain had been instrumental in the Munich Agreement. Chamberlain had met with Hitler; they had discussed and reached an agreement. The Prime Minister had declared to the world they had averted war and, thanks to him, there would be no war.

After Hitler reneged on the agreement, Chamberlain was made out to be a fool, and Winston Churchill became Prime Minister by 1940. The term "appeasement" came to mean Chamberlain and failure. However, ten short years later, the world had forgotten that fact. The term "Cold War" entered the public lexicon.

The end of the war brought many changes, many of them good. There would be an explosion of marriages; a result of this would be the creation of the term "Baby-Boomer." Between 1946 and 1964, approximately 73 million children were born. There would be a boom in the housing industry, as well as the thousands of new schools built. With demobilization, millions of women who had joined the workforce during the war were displaced by returning soldiers. These women, through multiple messages in popular culture and the mass media, were encouraged to give up their jobs and return to roles in the home. Most women, however, "wished to keep their jobs, and thus women made up approximately one-third of the peacetime labor force."[54] This would mean that men, both married and single, would spend more hours in close proximity to women that were not their wives than to the women that were. Since Creation, men and women have had very defined roles. The 1950s would see this beginning to change.

Because men and women began spending more time together, the ways couples dated started changing as well. In the early 50s, the dating stayed relatively the same as it had been. The process began with the man wooing the girl. The girl never asked the guy out. Before the first date, he called her home. There, he would first talk to the parents. Once the date was arranged, he picked her up and met the parents. The typical median marriage age for men was 22.6 for men and 20.4 for women. This was down from 26.8 and 23.4, respectively.

The change had started, in part, because of the war. Later in the decade, this started to evolve. In the 1930s, dating was about picking the best "provider." This was due, in large part, because of the Depression. Girls would date "competitively." Guys would, therefore, attempt to become the best providers by competing for the best jobs. After the war, the economic boom meant that everyone got great jobs, and in essence, girls married as soon as possible. Hence, the drop.

This would have an effect on later generations; high school, middle school, and even elementary children would begin to pair off. Subsequently, thirteen-year-olds who did not yet date were called "late daters." A 1961 study found that "40 percent of the fifth-graders in one middle-class Pennsylvania district were already dating."[55] Future generations would also learn that dating also made premarital sex permissible.

God and Schools

> *Those who don't know history are doomed to repeat it.*[56]
> —Edmund Burke

One of the most debated issues of the last two hundred years is prayer in schools. The other side argues that we are pushing religion and most parents in the western world think of this as a marriage between government, be it a monarchy, a democracy, or a representative republic, and the church. If parents are believers, they must demonstrate and capably explain to their children what the duty of a believer means.

We are also to infuse our conversations with our children, our love of and for our Father, and of others.

Prayers During the School Day

Initially, schools operated much as home, or even families did, in a Christ-centered way. After the kids arrived, "opening exercises began with the Lord's Prayer, Bible readings, and roll call."[57] When schools were founded, they would begin in a one-room schoolhouse, but this would be the practice even as the school expanded. During the 17th and 18th centuries, it would not be unusual to study the lives of martyrs. The New England Primer would talk about "Mr. John Roberts, Minister of the Gospel in London...was burnt at Smithfield, February 14th, 1554 (and) died courageously for the Gospel of Jesus Christ."[58] The books' original publication would include a picture of the current President of the United States, George Washington. It is no surprise, as the United States was founded on the abovementioned documents and was thus infused with Scripture.

It would be Massachusetts, as the seat of where the Pilgrims would land, that would create the first education law. Named the Old Deluder Satan Law of 1647, it stated that the purpose of education was: "It being one chief project of that old deluder, Satan, to keep men from the knowledge of the Scriptures."[59] This would be the understanding of not only the Saints but to anyone who has studied Scripture.

God's Idea of School

We are told to "Train up a child in the way he should go: and when he is old, he will not depart from it" (Proverbs 22:6, KJV). If we are to instruct our children, and we are, it is therefore not a leap that the hours they spend away from us for education would also involve some biblical teaching. Many in the west and throughout the world dislike the United States' heavy-handedness in dealing with other countries. Many feel it has become entangled in everyone's activities.

However, the American Founding Fathers used both the Magna Carta and the Pilgrims Mayflower Compact to define the new country. While it would be the Magna Carta that would give the idea that "first, that we have granted to God, and by this present charter have confirmed for us and our heirs in perpetuity...no free man shall be seized or imprisoned, or stripped of his rights or possessions, or outlawed or exiled, or deprived of his standing in any other way, nor will we proceed with force against him, or send others to do so, except by the lawful judgement of his equals or by the law of the land."[60] The idea of "all being equal under God" would be used by the American founders in its documents. The other document used was the Mayflower Compact.

The Compact says its mission was "undertaken, for the glory of God, and advancement of the Christian faith, and honour of our king and country, a voyage to plant the first colony in the Northerne parts of Virginia...by virtue hereof to enacte, constitute, and frame such just and equall laws, ordinances, acts, constitutions, and offices, from time to time, as shall be thought most meete and convenient for the generall good of the Colonie unto which we promise all due submission and obedience."[61] The ideas in these documents would form the basis for every representative republic that would follow.

In 1954, when President Dwight Eisenhower signed the Executive Order that added "Under God" to the United States National Anthem, he would say,

> From this day forward, the millions of our school children will daily proclaim in every city and town, every village and rural schoolhouse, the dedication of our nation and our

people to the Almighty. To anyone who truly loves America, nothing could be more inspiring than to contemplate this rededication of our youth, on each school morning, to our country's true meaning...In this way we are reaffirming the transcendence of religious faith in America's heritage and future; in this way we shall constantly strengthen those spiritual weapons which forever will be our country's most powerful resource, in peace or in war."[62]

The schools, as originally created, or even in the 1950s, are vastly different than those today.

Man's Idea of School

Since the 19th century, the education system has been eroded by a mindset that wants to prove that God has no place there. Compare the United Kingdom from the 17th century to today. In 1698 a group of five friends resolved to form a society "to communicate the Christian faith to a wide audience through education and the provision of Christian resources."[63] The Society for Promoting Christian Knowledge Schools would later include branches throughout Europe, Australia, and the United States. The Society was to use Scripture as one of its reading materials, as well as many other resources needed to spread the Gospel. The Society would initially have an incredible reach and influence until God began to be minimized in society. The Society would suffer because of what would be called secularism. Secularism champions "universal human rights above religious demands. It upholds equality laws that protect women, LGBT people, and minorities from religious discrimination. These equality laws ensure that non-believers have the same rights as those who identify with a religious or philosophical belief."[64] This is done by undermining people's beliefs that a belief in God means only rights for some.

This would be part of the gradual erosion of a belief system that was created during the Creation when, according to the first chapter of Genesis, "God created mankind in His own image." This means everything He believes; we believe. Since the Fall, Satan has spent his life using his deceitful nature to turn us from God. This is done by using wrapping lies in a little bit of truth. This means that many now believe that "universal rights" are different than "Universal Rights." The Apostle Paul tells us that "For all have sinned and fall short of the glory of God" (Romans 3:23, NIV), and "all" would mean that God has Universal Rights.

Scripture has long since been a part of education and, up until the 19th century, was used throughout the world to not only teach them to read and instill a habit of reading from the Bible but also to help guide them in their thinking during very important years.

However, beginning in the 19th century, the western world began a slow descent away from God. You could still read stories about "200,000 clergy, many crucified, scalped and otherwise tortured, were killed during the approximately sixty years of communist rule in the former Soviet Union,"[65] however, it is becoming more common to see reports of "twice as many 12th graders in 2010–13 reported "never" attending services (21%) compared to 1976–79 (10%)."[66] Before the 20th century, countries would shut down on the Sabbath; by the middle of the last century, businesses were opened, and farmers were spending the Lord's Day in the fields.

This is the result of schools that have moved away from a biblical foundation, and if they even teach what they call "religious education," "parents can withdraw their children for all or part of the lessons."[67] This would mean that parents who don't see the knowledge of Scripture and God important are ensuring that future generations will move closer to the "father of lies."

CHAPTER SEVEN

The 1960s

The 1960s was the beginning of a social, political, and moral split that would affect every part of life. The decade would include major riots, assassinations, a deepening war involvement, and the idea that no one in charge can be trusted. Like no decade before, the events that took place in the 1960s are still affecting us today.

At the dawn of the sixties, in 1958, Chinese Communist Party (CCP) Chairman Mao Zedong implanted what he called his Five Year Plan. Also called the Great Step Forward, it helped establish for the entire country detailed economic development guidelines which included transferring more property to collective ownership. The Political Bureau of the CPC had determined that the gross value of agricultural products should increase 270 percent; therefore, part of the plan included encouraging economic growth, cultivating cultural and scientific development, and strengthening national defense. Instead of 270 percent, 35 percent was achieved.

However, much of what Mao wanted to do was suppress the growing Christian population. The Chinese government has always had an adversarial relationship with Christians. Because Christianity goes against much of the communist teaching, Buddhism is China's widely practiced religion. Buddhism does not "include the idea of worshipping a creator god...the basic tenets of Buddhist teaching are straightforward and practical: nothing is fixed or permanent."[68] It would not be until the 1970s and the death of Mao that Christianity began to thrive in China.

José María Velasco Ibarra would become president of Ecuador in 1960. As would happen in all but one of his four terms, he would be removed by a military coup. However, before he was removed in 1961, he would nullify the Rio de Janeiro Protocol. This agreement, signed in 1942, ended the territorial war between Ecuador and Peru. The hostilities would continue, with major wars in the 1980s and 1990s.

John Fitzgerald Kennedy would become the 35th president of the United States in 1961. His charm and charisma, along with that of his wife Jackie and their children, would captivate most of the west. His assassination in November 1963, the subsequent theories about his assassin(s) and coverups began the erosion of confidence in the American people in their leaders. It can be argued that if Kennedy had not been killed, the

United States' involvement in what became known as the Vietnam War would have been limited.

The race wars that had been escalating in American cities would climax in 1968 with the assassination of Dr. Martin Luther King, Jr. It wasn't just the United States that were having race wars; the sixties would see race wars in Pakistan, Indonesia, Singapore, the United Kingdom, and Australia. For all the time and money we have invested, since racial wars are continuing to escalate, the Organization of the Petroleum Exporting Countries (OPEC) was created. OPEC is basically a union of thirteen countries that accounts for roughly eighty percent of the oil reserves. This means OPEC can and does control the price of oil. This would be important because now, with both husbands and wives working. A lesson the world would learn all too well in the 1970s.

The idea of the No-Fault Divorce that had been created at the end of the Revolution in 1917 had slowly worked its way into other countries. Starting in China in 1950, it would move to Canada, Australia, the United States, Mexico, Germany, Spain, and Sweden.

Before this idea was introduced, a reason had to be given for divorce. The most common reasons of the time were adultery, bigamy, or mental illness. However, any of the reasons given could be argued. The no-fault divorce indicated to everyone involved, the attorneys, the judges, the participants, the children, society at large, and even the church, that marriage was no longer a priority. People are, for the most part, lazy creatures, and if it seems easier to divorce than to stay married, then that is what they will do. The divorce rate climbed to "26 percent by 1967....Slowly, other states adopted no-fault divorce, and couples were able to split on the basis of irreconcilable differences."[69] While this would be a massive jump, the divorce rate would never be this low again.

Once women started to move into the workplace and spend more time away from home, a major breakdown of God's design occurred. The Movement of the '60s and '70s is called the Second Feminist Wave, as the first wave happened in the 1910s and '20s and pushed women's suffrage. The Second Wave pushed for much more. In the guise of "equality in the workplace," the effort was made to place them as equals in every respect with men.

One of those responsible for the Second Wave was Simone de Beauvoir. De Beauvoir could be seen as one of the first modern women. She was born on January 9, 1908, at the 6th arrondissement of Paris, France. She would become one of the strongest advocates for abortion. But also advocate for the breakdown of the family, saying that women shouldn't even have the choice of staying home with the kids. She would deny the presence of God, calling Christian values the "values of ambiguity."[70] Her primary argument would be, one of the first of its time, that there is a distinction between sex and gender by arguing that "one is not born but becomes a woman."[71] De Beauvoir's work, *The Second Sex*, would lay the groundwork for Betty Friedan's *The Feminine Mystique*. *The Mystique*, published in 1963, argued that to achieve what she called "feminism fulfillment" was for women to say, "I want something more than my husband and my children and my home."[72] Suddenly, instead of wanting a husband and being a housewife, women were being told that that was not enough. They would begin to be told the lie that they could "have it all." This would force women to choose between a "career" and a "family," which, of course, is not what God intended.

Lastly, Friedan would become the first president of the National Organization of Women (NOW); while she was the face of the feminist organization, Pauli Murray would have more of an impact on the future. Murray would be an openly gay African American woman. Murray was born on November 20, 1910, in Baltimore, Maryland, and over her seventy-five years, she would be an attorney, author, and a civil rights activist. However, her biggest impact would be as an ordained priest. In 1977, she became the first woman ordained in the Episcopal Church. She is honored each year by the Episcopal Church for "her work to address injustice and promote reconciliation between races, sexes, and economic classes through her work as an attorney, writer, feminist, poet and educator."[73] This militant, openly gay priest being celebrated by any organization can not call itself a church.

God and Justice

Many that live deserve death. And some that die deserve life. Can you give it to them? Then do not be too eager to deal out death in judgement. For even the very wise cannot see all ends.[74]

—J. R. R. Tolkien

In the current world situation, the word "justice" has been misconstrued to mean something totally different. God *is* Justice. He is Right. He is Truth. How can Right and Truth not be Justice?

To begin, we need to understand some terms. Truth is a "verified or indisputable fact, proposition, principle, or the like."[75] To be right is to be "correct."[76] Finally, justice is "the quality of being just; righteousness, equitableness, or moral rightness."[77] How does this compare to what Scripture says? To this question, Jesus answered, "I am the way and the truth and the life. No one comes to the Father except through me" (John 14:6,

NIV). This is the key. Jesus is all of those, the Way, the Truth, and the Life. Therefore, Jesus must be Justice.

Prayers for Justice

The Book of Ecclesiastes is written by King Solomon, calling himself the preacher. King Solomon was the son of King David. There are many biblical figures that even atheists begrudgingly admit are real. King Solomon is one of them.

Scripture identifies him as the builder of the First Temple. He is portrayed as great in wisdom, wealth, and power beyond either of the previous kings of the country. Solomon knew his wisdom came from God. He could have asked God for anything; he asked for wisdom so that he could be a wise ruler. As is always the case, He gives us more than we ask if we earnestly pray. God's answer was:

> 'Since you have asked for this and not for long life or wealth for yourself, nor have asked for the death of your enemies but for discernment in administering justice, I will do what you have asked. I will give you a wise and discerning heart, so that there will never have been anyone like you, nor will there ever be. Moreover, I will give you what you have not

> asked for—both wealth and honor—so that in your lifetime you will have no equal among kings. And if you walk in obedience to me and keep my decrees and commands as David your father did, I will give you a long life.' Then Solomon awoke—and he realized it had been a dream.
>
> 1 Kings 3:11–15 (NIV)

By the time he wrote Ecclesiastes, Solomon had quite possibly attained everything possible under the sun.

He had more money than anyone ever had before, and few people have since. It is estimated that King Solomon collected over $1,000,000,000,000 each year in tax collections. That does not take into account the property he owned. He would rule over thousands of square miles. He would have seven hundred wives and three hundred concubines. By every comparable method, he had not only been a greater ruler than his father, but by the end of his life, he knew "God will bring into judgment both the righteous and the wicked, for there will be a time for every activity, a time to judge every deed" (Ecclesiastes 3:17, NIV). His conclusion was that everything was meaningless if it was not God-centered.

God's Ideas of Justice

There are many examples in Scripture about God and justice. One Psalmist would declare that "Righteousness and justice are the foundation of your throne; love and faithfulness go before you" (Psalm 89:14, NIV). God and justice are the same. This means that there are absolute truths.

To put it into an idea that even a small child can understand, an absolute truth would be that night is always dark. To know the absolute truth, we are to study Scripture and pray, "Teach me your ways, O LORD, that I may live according to your truth!" (Psalm 86:11, NLT). The more we study Scripture, the more we can be like Him.

The Bible is full of God's rules of how He wants us to live. Just a short list includes the Ten Commandments, the laws that are covered in the Book of Romans, and what Jesus would call the "greatest commandments."

> 'Love the Lord your God with all your heart and with all your soul and with all your mind and with all your strength.' The second is this: 'Love your neighbor as yourself.' There is no commandment greater than these.
>
> Mark 12:30–31 (NIV)

All of these mean that we are to put others before ourselves.

Man's Idea of Justice

Every western civilization has laws based, at least in part, on the Ten Commandments. It is illegal to kill and to steal. There are laws that protect children and those who can't defend themselves.

When the Pilgrims landed on the North American continent, they signed what would become known as the Mayflower Compact. The compact would read, "In the name of God, amen. We...by these Presents, solemnly and mutually, in the Presence of God and one another, covenant and combine ourselves together into a civil Body Politick, for our better Ordering and Preservation, and Furtherance of the Ends aforesaid: And by Virtue hereof do enact, constitute, and frame, such just and equal Laws, Ordinances, Acts, Constitutions, and Officers."[78] This was a simple agreement between themselves, but since they had left both England and Holland being faithful, it was also their covenant with God. The idea expressed would be used in many governing documents.

The United States would have the Declaration of Independence, which would say that "All men are created equal, that they are endowed by their Creator with certain unalienable Rights, that among these are Life, Liberty and the pursuit of Happiness. That to secure these rights, Governments are instituted among Men, deriving their just powers from the consent of the governed."[79] Hundreds of countries would follow this in the intervening two centuries.

One example is the kingdom of Lesotho. Lesotho is a landlocked country that is entirely surrounded by South Africa. It became a country in 1966 and, as of 2018, had a population of 2,285,392 million. Ninety percent of the population of Lesotho is Christian.

Unfortunately, also over the same two centuries, we as believers have allowed secular thinking to erode every part of our life.

For example, the European Union (EU) was created in the 1950s with the "aim of ending the frequent and bloody wars between neighbours...(and) to secure lasting peace."[80] Apparently, wars are prevented, and peace is maintained by "inclusion, tolerance, justice, solidarity, and non-discrimination."[81] While inclusion and solidarity would sound like ideas that everyone should be in agreement with.

The problem is what many have done to convince us that inclusion and solidarity are the opposite of what they really mean. Today inclusion means that we must accept homosexuality and every other sexual deviancy as "normal." We must accept criminal behavior, be it murder, extortion, property destruction, or a list that continues to grow, in the name of "social justice."

One example is the Black Panther group that formed in the 1960s. The Black Panther Party (BPP), originally the Black Panther Party for Self-Defense, was a political organization founded by college students Bobby Seale and Huey P. Newton in 1966. It was created, in many ways, for "justice." In this instance, justice for blacks. They were, in many ways, the precursor of today's Black Lives Matter (BLM) movement.

Founded under what would be called its Ten Points document, it demanded, among other ideas, that "we want an immediate end to police brutality…(and) we want decent education for our people that exposes the true nature of this decadent American society."[82] It is hard to argue with either of those ideas; it is easy to see how they morphed to become Defund the Police and Critical Race Theory. By the early '70s, the BPP would have chapters in numerous major cities and international chapters in Britain and Algeria.

Although attendance would dissipate as the seventies became the eighties, the BPP and its members would find other ways to implement those ideas. Some of them would become elected officials; others would become ministers; still, others would infiltrate schools. In every area of life, individuals, regardless of race, would be bombarded with the ideas advanced in the Ten Points. The validity of the information no longer matters as it has become the reasoning behind so much social upheaval. This would be added to the others who had already infiltrated and were systematically dismantling the foundations of everyday life.

CHAPTER EIGHT

The 1970s

The 1970s was called the "pivot of change" for every western country. The social and political upheavals that followed the end of the postwar economic boom continued. The United Kingdom elected its first female Prime Minister, Margaret Thatcher. This would be viewed as part of the Feminist Movement.

Once women started to move into the workplace and spend more time away from home, a major breakdown of God's design occurred. The 1960s would see the invention of the birth control pill, which would usher in the sexual revolution of the 1970s.

By the mid-1960s, the pill and other contraceptives were gaining popularity, but they were only legal for married couples. In 1972, they became legal for unmarried couples as well.

By the end of the 1960s, Great Britain had legalized abortion. Most of the western world followed shortly thereafter, with it becoming acceptable in the United States with the passage of Roe V. Wade in 1973. The court case would be groundbreaking as it not only argued that women had the right to choose an abortion but also "the abortion right is not absolute. It must be balanced against the government's interests in protecting women's health and prenatal life."[83] This meant that those who opposed abortion would find the idea harder to argue if it was to "protect a woman's health."

The church would undergo a wide variety of changes, in essence, because society was undergoing a wide variety of changes. The birth control pill appeared in the early 1960s. The approval of birth control played a major role in the sexual liberation of women that took place during the 1960s. For the first time, women were free to enjoy spontaneous sex without fear of pregnancy. Today, it's estimated that more than 10 million women use the pill.

Nineteen seventy would see the first Earth Day. The idea that we are so powerful that we can destroy God's creation was created by an activist. The initial idea behind this was a teach-in, to use the riot mentality that was sweeping across college campuses and get them to protest the damage we were doing to the planet. That first year, 20 million Americans took part in the Green Day event. That was ten percent of the total population at the time. Those millions took "to the streets, parks, and auditoriums to demonstrate against the impacts of 150 years of industrial development which had left a growing legacy of serious human health impacts."⁸⁴ In the fifty years since its founding, the Earth Day Organization, "over 95 percent of primary and secondary schools in the US and millions of schools globally observe Earth Day each year...(they provide) students with the knowledge and skills to build environmental and climate literacy."⁸⁵ Although, neither the environment nor the climate can be literate. But since what words mean have slowly been redefined, not many people realize that.

OPEC would declare an oil shortage for much of the decade, thanks in part to the Yom Kippur War and the Iranian Revolution. This shortage would affect the United States, Canada, Western Europe, Australia, and New Zealand. However, one event in the United States that caused more controversy than anything else centered around the idea of forgiveness.

Forgiveness, in all of the teachings of Jesus, is one of the toughest. It's tough to do on a one-time basis; it's almost impossible to do on a day-to-day basis. One example of forgiveness can be seen in United States President Jerry Ford and his pardon of former president Richard Nixon. Ford was born in July 1913 and made history as both the first unelected vice president and president of the United States. This happened because of Watergate.

For those born after Watergate, it is hard to imagine how much it transformed the country. As hard as it may be to believe now, before Watergate, most Americans had respect for and trusted their government.

The last major scandal involving a president was the Tea Pot Dome Scandal in the early 1920s. President Warren G. Harding's Secretary of the Interior Albert B. Fall received $100,000 worth of bribes. Harding died in office before the scandal broke, no one else was ever indicted, and the evidence does not point to Harding benefitting from or even knowing about the scandal.

Much as Kennedy would be a hero during World War II, Ford was one as well. The difference was that Ford did not publicize the events that made him the hero the way Kennedy did. In May 1943, Ford was assigned to the USS *Monterey*. While he was on board, *Monterey* participated in many actions in the Pacific with the Third and Fifth Fleets during the Fall of 1943 and in 1944.

During this time, it was damaged by a typhoon and by a fire that started during the storm. During the storm, the ship "rolled twenty-five degrees which caused Ford to lose his footing and slide toward the edge of the deck. The two-inch steel ridge around the edge of the carrier slowed him enough so he could roll and twist into the catwalk below the deck. As he later stated, 'I was lucky; I could have easily gone overboard.'"[86] Jerry Ford was always who he was in every situation, almost unheard of occurrence for a thirty-year politician. The same could not be said for Nixon, who seemed to have a sliding moral compass depending on who he was with and the issues covered. We tend to see the world as we see others; that is, we think that everyone thinks like we do, so Nixon tended to see the world as a big conspiracy; Ford, however, believed that people could work together.

I believe Ford knew from his first weekend in August 1974 when he assumed the presidency that he would have to pardon Nixon.

He also knew it would be sooner rather than later, and he kept waiting for America to come around to his way of thinking. He mentioned the possibility of a pardon in his first press conference on August 28, nineteen days after becoming president. When asked if he would pardon Nixon, he responded, "I am not ruling it out. It is an option and a proper option for any president."[87] It would take him another ten days from this first press conference to his pardon announcement. With that announcement, Ford was telling us to move on, put Watergate behind us, and move on. However, as we all know, offering forgiveness and moving on is something extremely difficult to do.

Ford would be the first United States president since William McKinley in the 1900s that didn't use God as a prop in a speech. Even though there had been many opportunities in the intervening seventy years, public servants had been, for a long time, standing on what Ford would call the "shifting sands of situation ethics." He would say that,

> Jesus said, 'What is a man profited, if he shall gain the whole world and lose his own soul?' We stand in danger today of losing the soul of America to the seductions of material gain and moral apathy, to a new code of conduct which reviles the basic truths and mocks the fundamental beliefs on which this Nation and much of religion were founded. Public officials have a special responsibility to set a good example for others to follow, in both their private and public conduct. The American people, particularly our young people, cannot be expected to take pride or even to participate in a system of government that is defiled and dishonored, whether in the White House or in the halls of Congress. Jesus said, 'Unto whomsoever much is given, of him shall much be required.' Personal integrity is not too much to ask of public servants. We should accept nothing less. The American people have seen too much abuse of the moral imperatives of honesty and of decency upon which religion and government, and civilized society must rest. To remedy these abuses,

we must look not only to the government but, more importantly, to the Bible, the church, the human heart.[88]

Whether we agree with Ford politically or not, it can not be argued that he was prophetic in his predictions of moral values being undermined and of the consequences that it has had.

God and Forgiveness

If we really want to love, we must learn how to forgive.[89]

—Mother Teresa

The entirety of the Bible is based on forgiveness. The Fall brought sin into the world through our disobedience. The whole reason for our existence is to fellowship with God. Believing Satan instead of God, we brought sin into the world, corrupting everything, even our relationship with Him.

What is God's solution? To forgive us. He could have either abandoned us or destroyed us. Instead, He removed the sin, "As far as the east is from the west, so far has he removed our transgressions from us" (Psalm 103:12, NIV). There have been many times in my past that I have turned my back on people who have wronged me; instead of forgiving them, I just forgot them.

Prayers for Forgiveness

There are hundreds of examples of forgiveness in Scripture, but one that shows it perfectly is when Jesus hung on the cross and He prayed, "Father, forgive them; for they know not what they do" (Luke 23:34, KJV). After being scourged, spit on, having ails driven through His hands and feet, mocked Him, been abandoned and denied by even His followers. But yet, He asked for forgiveness for everyone.

The phrase "forgive and forget" does not appear in Scripture, although this is the idea that is expressed in literature. Although He shows us how to forgive and forget as far as our sins are concerned, for He removes them, "As far as the east is from the west, so far has he removed our transgressions from us" (Psalm 103:12, NIV). The issue of forgiveness is too often brushed over, and other solutions are given.

Without forgiveness, we would be going to hell. How important is the grudge against a neighbor or a coworker when looked at that way?

CHAPTER NINE

The 1980s

The 1980s would be a decade with many cultural events. From the collapse of the Soviet Union to the collapse of the Berlin Wall. From the birth of rap music to the birth of music television.

One of the biggest cultural events would be the introduction of the twenty-four-hour news cycle. On June 1, 1980, the Cable News Network (CNN) was launched by Robert Edward Turner III, known as Ted. Turner was born November 1938 in Cincinnati, Ohio. Before starting the fledging cable channel, Turner bought both radio and television stations. He essentially started CNN because he was told it. When it signed on, the lead story was "about the attempted assassination of civil rights leader Vernon Jordan."[90] While the attempt was newsworthy, the twenty-four-hour news cycle made the most non-newsworthy item newsworthy, simply for the fact that there was time to fill.

It would become so successful it would have several clones in North America and other continents. There is even a CNN International, which would focus on world events. Staying up to date on news and other popular events of the day is never a bad idea. However, all people have a built-in bias, and most broadcasters are liberal. That means the news that is broadcast most of that twenty-four-hour cycle is an attack on the values that created the United States.

Nineteen eighty-one would see the birth of Music Television (MTV). Although music broadcast on television was not new, this was different. MTV sold music, but it largely sold sex. In the early years, it promoted the videos and thus condoned the performances of Madonna, Prince, and Duran Duran, and dozens more like them. These people were not musicians; they were flesh peddlers.

The 1980s would see the invention of the internet. The computer had been invented several decades before, but on January 1, 1983, the "ARPAnet adopted TCP/IP protocols which enabled data exchange between different computers."[91] Neither computers nor the internet is bad, but it would be what they would be used for in the coming decades. Initially, it was used to unite friends and families through emails, photos, and videos. That would change into ways to divide the family as even members of the same household spend hours upon hours staring at different screens as each member of the family played games, watched movies, or worked online. Family time ceased to be "together time."

By the late 1970s, a new pope would be appointed. He was born Karol Józef Wojtyła in May 1920, in Wadowice, Poland, but the world would know him as Pope John Paul II. He would go on to become the second longest-serving pope of all time. He would say,

> I understand that I have to lead Christ's church into the Third Millennium through prayer, by various programs. But I saw that this is not enough...Why? Precisely because the family is threatened, the family is under attack.[92]

The Pope understood that family was not just earthly definition, but the heavenly one. One of the things he would go on the offensive against was Communism.

He would be one of several world leaders that would attack Communism during the 1980s. Another individual that would do so would be United States President Ronald Reagan. Reagan was born in February 1911 in Tampico, Illinois. He would go from being a Hollywood to California governor. Along the way, he would become a fierce opponent of Communism and the Soviet Union. He would say at a college commencement in 1982 that,

> The Soviet Union is a huge empire ruled by an elite that holds all power and all privilege, and they hold it tightly because…they fear the infectiousness of even a little freedom, and because of this in many ways their system has failed. The Soviet empire is faltering because it is rigid—centralized control has destroyed incentives for innovation, efficiency, and individual achievement. Spiritually, there is a sense of malaise and resentment.[93]

But President Reagan, when talking about how those who choose to worship the state instead of God, would say,

> Without God, there is no virtue, because there's no prompting of the conscience. Without God, we're mired in the material, that flat world that tells us only what the senses perceive. Without God, there is a coarsening of the society. And without God, democracy will not and cannot long endure. If we ever forget that we're one nation under God, then we will be a nation gone under.[94]

He would be a divorced movie actor, two of the things that would lead many to question his Christianity. However, he would be the last American president to mention God, except in passing, for the remainder of the 20th century.

The third of the trifecta that had as her mission defeating communism would be Prime Minister Margaret Thatcher. Margaret Hilda Thatcher (née Roberts) was born on October 1925 in Grantham, Lincolnshire, and would become Prime Minister of the United Kingdom from 1979 to 1990 and Leader of the Conservative Party from 1975 to 1990. She was the longest-serving British prime minister of the 20th century and the first woman to hold that office. She would work effectively with both Reagan and Pope John Paul. The first female Prime Minister would say, "The pursuit of equality itself is a mirage. What's more desirable and more practicable than the pursuit of equality is the pursuit of equality of opportunity."[95] By the 1990s, Thatcher's successor was Tony Blair. Blair was similar in many ways to United States president Bill Clinton. When Blair was asked about his faith, he would say simply, "We don't do God."[96] However, Thatcher did.

In many of her speeches, she spoke of her faith very openly. From one, that many called her "Sermon on the Mount Speech," she said,

> We were made in God's own image and, therefore, we are expected to use all our own power

of thought and judgement in exercising that choice; and further, that if we open our hearts to God, He has promised to work within us. And third, that Our Lord Jesus Christ, the Son of God, when faced with His terrible choice and lonely vigil *chose* to lay down His life that our sins may be forgiven.[97]

If many of the leaders in the intervening six decades had been believers and had shared their faith, the world might not have slipped so far from the church.

However, church membership continued to drop. By the 1980s, "66 percent of traditionalists—US adults born before 1946—belong to a church."[98] It would be the same in Europe as well as "attendance statistics at Church of England services still showed that numbers dropped off markedly during the 1980s and into the 1990s."[99] In only eight centuries, a minuscule time in relation to the world, membership had dropped roughly thirty percent in America and by two-thirds in Europe.

Unfortunately, it would never be this high again.

God and the Church

Prayer will make a man cease from sin, or sin will entice a man to cease from prayer.[100]

—John Bunyan

This chapter should not be necessary. The church should be the last place we try to show our authority over God. However, at least since the days of the Roman Empire, man has been fighting God for control, turning it from the Church, uppercase "C," to church, lowercase "c."

Prayers for the Church

We are to hold each other accountable. We are told that,

> If the whole…community sins unintentionally and does what is forbidden in any of the LORD's commands, even though the community is unaware of the matter, when they realize their guilt and the sin they committed becomes known, the assembly must…present it before the tent of meeting.
> Leviticus 4:13–14 (NIV)

Also, "If anyone sins because they do not speak up when they hear a public charge to testify regarding something they have seen or learned about, they will be held responsible" (Leviticus 5:1, NIV). This is to be the rule if the people we see sinning are believers, nonbelievers, political leaders, or church leaders.

This is extremely difficult to do since no one wants an honest appraisal of their lives reflected on them. As sons and daughters of the Living God, we are all one family. Don't you advise, sometimes strongly advise, your family about choices they're making or paths they are following?

God's Idea of the Church

The covenant made in the New Testament is spoken most effectively by the Apostle Peter when Jesus asks him who He is, "You are the Messiah, the Son of the living God" (Matthew 16:16, NIV) To this, Jesus replied that on that rock, "I will build my church; and the gates of hell shall not prevail against it" (Matthew 16:18, NIV). This "rock" that He was the Son of the Living God would be as revolutionary in roughly AD 30 as the Old Testament covenant with Abraham was.

The rules concerning worship that God had given to Aaron had been replaced by endless rules that did little but gave Pharisees a lot of power and a lot of wealth. This new dynamic would give everyone, rich or poor, educated or illiterate, immediate access to God through Jesus.

Man's Idea of Church

Just as the Garden of Eden was the beginning of the Old Testament, Jesus' ministry was the beginning of the New. Also, just like in the Old Testament, man was given one job. We were not to eat the fruit in the Garden, and yet we did. In the New Testament, our only job was to follow God, "Follow me, and I will make you fishers of men" (Matthew 4:19, KJV). Just like in the Old Testament, we couldn't obey. We took the Good News and corrupted it. God knew this in the beginning and would send Jesus to erase the Fall, and He will return to replace the church that has taken the place of His Church.

What began as the Church became the church. The church has been the target of churches since the beginning of Jesus' ministry. Originally, it was the Sadducees and Pharisees; then, it was the Roman Empire. After His Ascension, the church would face challenges from both within and without. The church would slowly begin to take control of itself in the form of legalism.

Legalism can be defined as a "strict, literal, or excessive conformity to the law or to a religious or moral code."[101] It was this same adherence to the "rules" that the Pharisees served. Jesus warned us that,

> The teachers of the law and the Pharisees sit in Moses' seat. So you must be careful to do

everything they tell you. But do not do what they do, for they do not practice what they preach. They tie up heavy, cumbersome loads and put them on other people's shoulders, but they themselves are not willing to lift a finger to move them.

Matthew 23:2–4 (NIV)

Yet, it was this legalism, some call dogma, that has worked its way into Christianity ever since.

This legalism stranglehold is why many stay away from organized religion, and why many would leave the organized churches because they felt, as the Pilgrims did, that the church "had strayed beyond Christ's teachings, and established religious rituals, and church hierarchies, that went against the teachings of the Bible."[102] This would lead to the Mayflower Compact.

This is another example of God's Word being used for His glory. The Mayflower Compact and the Great Awakening that would follow would cause a series of revivals to begin around the world and would result in the conversions of hundreds of thousands of souls. Those revivals are still continuing.

This idea of the church or the Church is a constant struggle.

CHAPTER TEN

The 1990s

Before I begin this chapter, I want to share something. This chapter contains some sensitive material as it deals with how sex has permeated and, in many ways, become the dominant thing that drives society. I include this idea in the 1990s decade instead of the 1960s because of one individual, William Jefferson Blythe. After his mother remarried and his stepfather adopted him, he would become Bill Clinton and would eventually become the 42nd president of the United States.

In the years after he left office, many books were written about what a vile and debase person he was. However, there were rumors, both confirmed and unconfirmed, about his nature before his election. In many ways, we, as believers, are responsible for the moral decline that has happened since because we did not have enough courage to put forth an individual of strong moral character.

We also were too prudish (or use a different word if you want) to explain to people why Clinton's behavior was so disgusting.

Because of our failings, he became the leader of the most powerful country in the world. When it was determined how he spent much of his time, the fact that there was so little backlash would send a loud and clear signal to other leaders, married couples, singles, kids, churches, everyone that a weak moral character is no big deal.

I have written the following chapter with as much sensitivity as possible.

What is love? Love is one of those words that is has been so overused. The word is used to express a like for everything. People say, "I love ice cream," or "I love my dog." We love our new shoes, a new pasta dish, or a song on the radio. Once a word becomes this common, it loses what makes it special. Think of this example. We read in Matthew that "You are the salt of the earth. But if the salt loses its saltiness, how can it be made salty again? It is no longer good for anything, except to be thrown out and trampled underfoot" (Matthew 5:13, NIV). So then, what gives love its "saltiness"?

Love is the most sacred of all things. It is the *one thing* that everyone desires. The problem is the world has redefined love and has replaced it with the word "sex."

We all know that love and sex are two completely different things. Whereas love can lead to sex, it doesn't work the other way. Unfortunately, many use sex. Many sell sex as a commodity. The same cannot be said about love; love is not sold. That's how you know they are not the same.

Believers know the difference. Many non-believers know the difference as well. The problem is that the lie is being perpetrated on the children. They don't know the difference. One of the biggest stories of the 1990s was trying to explain to children how one of the phrases at the time, "It's only sex," was such an immoral one.

It began on January 20, 1993. At twelve o'clock eastern time, Bill Clinton was sworn into office. President Clinton, a serial adulterer, had run a campaign against George Herbert Walker Bush. The contrast between the two could not have been more clear. Clinton had avoided the draft; Bush was a World War II military hero. Clinton discussed the type of underwear he wore; Bush ran on family values. Over the course of his campaign, many, many stories had leaked out about Clinton. Stories about how he, while Governor of Arkansas, used the state police as nothing short of pimps. Stories about him being someone who never took no for an answer.

The stories were ignored, even by many believers, and Clinton would win. Clinton would receive 370 electoral votes to Bush's 168. However, the deciding factor would be the third-party candidate, Texas businessman H. Ross Perot. While he would not receive any electoral votes, he would receive 18 percent of the votes. Speculation at the time was that Clinton and Perot were working together to ensure his election. The fact that Perot would only run one more time, in 1996 during Clinton's reelection, only added to the rumors.

The story that would lead to Clinton's impeachment began in 1995. It was then that forty-nine-year-old Clinton began an affair with the twenty-two-year-old White House intern Monica Lewinsky. It ended in 1997 and only came to light when a different sexual allegation was being investigated. He would address the allegations at the end of a speech to, sadly, children and educators. He would say,

> But I want to say one thing to the American people. I want you to listen to me. I'm going to say this again. I did not have sexual relations with that woman, Miss Lewinsky. I never told anybody to lie, not a single time—never. These allegations are false.[103]

The investigation would be followed by millions and would give many lurid details.

The Impeachment Trial would become so embarrassing that Clinton would play a word game. When asked if he is having a relationship with Lewinsky, he responded,

> It depends on what the meaning of the word 'is' is. If the—if he—if 'is' means is and never has been, that is not—that is one thing. If it means there is none, that was a completely true statement...Now, if someone had asked me on that day, are you having any kind of sexual relations with Ms. Lewinsky, that is, asked me a question in the present tense, I would have said no. And it would have been completely true.[104]

Clinton would be impeached by the House of Representatives on December 19, 1998, by a vote of 228–206. However, just as would be done with President Andrew Johnson, the Senate failed to convict. Clinton's presidency ended quietly, but the damage had been done.

By the 1990s, rap music started becoming mainstream. It had been around before that. However, 1990 would make the music hard to get away from. That year would see the album *As Nasty As They Wanna Be* become the first-ever rap album to go platinum. The group, 2 Live Crew, would make history with a song called "Me So Horny." As all new music is, rap was targeted toward the kids. In the linear notes (the notes inside an album or cd cover), the group thanks Chris Jurewicz, one of their fans who had, at ten, written them a fan letter.

What should have happened was the church should have led the fight against the music industry. However, we had been taught over the last century to look to the state. So it was that the Parents Music Resource Center would be the ones who would "take on" the music industry. The Parents Music Resource Center was created by the wives of Washington DC politicians. I, along with some of my other colleagues, followed the lawsuit and the results closely. We were working on the radio as disc-jockeys. The two things we knew was that by one, giving rap music this much publicity, more children would be interested in it than would have been. Second, with this much publicity, more artists would begin to turn to rap.

Before rap, each generation discovers "new" music. Before rap, it was rock and roll. Before that, it was country or the blues. The younger generation is always looking for something new, and the more the older generation makes that something new look bad, the more it's wanted.

The obscenity trial that followed "proposed that record companies either cease the production of music with violent and sexually charged lyrics or develop a motion picture-style ratings system for albums."[105] The result would be the rating systems that would adorn future music releases. The worst offenders would rate an additional sticker that read "Parental Advisory: Explicit Lyrics." This last would guarantee that more musicians would want them.

One of the biggest news stories of the 1990s was the collapse of the wall between East Germany and West Germany. The wall was a barrier that physically and ideologically divided Berlin. It was built in 1961 by the German Democratic Republic (GDR, East Germany) and authorities officially referred to the Berlin Wall as the Anti-Fascist Protection Rampart. Before the wall was built, it was estimated that over three million Germans left East Germany into West Germany, where they were then free to travel to other parts of the world. This wall came to symbolize, in many ways, the Cold War itself. The East vs. West, imprisoned vs. free mentality, was memorialized by many. However, one of those whose speech has long been remembered, one from President Ronald Reagan.

In one of his speeches in 1987, he said,

> There is one sign the Soviets can make that would be unmistakable, that would advance dramatically the cause of freedom and peace. General Secretary Gorbachev, if you seek peace, if you seek prosperity for the Soviet Union and Eastern Europe, if you seek lib-

eralization: Come here to this gate! Mr. Gorbachev, open this gate! Mr. Gorbachev, tear down this wall![106]

With the leaders of the United States, Great Britain, and the Vatican all thanking God, the church leaders had a golden opportunity to show the world that the most powerful people in the world knew where their power came from. However, the church leaders were more concerned with other power.

Earthly power is, most of the time, tied to money. Church leaders had found a way to chase mega dollars while disguising it as a new way of reaching the unchurched. Starting in the 1950s, the word "megachurch" was created. One of the earliest ones in the United States was the Foursquare Church, founded in 1923 by Aimee Semple McPherson.

McPherson was born on October 9, 1890, in Salford, Ontario, Canada. In the 1920s and 1930s, she pioneered the use of modern media in religious services, using radio to draw on the growing appeal of popular entertainment and incorporating stage techniques into her weekly sermons. Other pastors saw how successful she was, and many of them showed how much money Foursquare brought in.

By the 1990s, many of the church leaders, pastors, deacons, etc., were choosing the franchise type of model, having one church "that just happens to meet in different locations. The different locations may have satellite uplink to the 'main church' or have their own pastoral system preaching the same type of message as presented in the 'main church.' The same leaders have oversight of both the main church and the 'satellite' churches."[107] This means that, in essence, each satellite church has a leader. There would also be multiple messages for children, which means multiple youth pastors. Multiple sites meant more pastors that worked with schools, worship pastors, more administrators. Each additional person required a salary. More everything, except God.

Just like in a household, or a business, the more expenses you have, the more income you need. The church had begun to be looked at as a business, so instead of God, money was soon what the leaders chased. To ensure an ever-increasing amount of income, the Word began to be watered down.

By 1990, "20.4 percent of the population attended an Orthodox Christian church on any given weekend."[108] Twenty percent! The church was the only remnant left from the Fall, and we were systematically dismantling it.

Since feminism began to go mainstream, women have been trying to find a way to replace men. The 1990s would provide that way with a sheep.

Dolly was a cloned sheep. She was "born" on July 5, 1996, and had three mothers. The first mother provided the egg, the other the DNA, and a third carried the cloned embryo to term. She was created using a technique called somatic cell nuclear transfer. In this process, the cell nucleus from an adult cell is transferred into an unfertilized oocyte (developing egg cell) that has had its cell nucleus removed. The hybrid cell is then stimulated to divide by an electric shock. After that, it's implanted in a surrogate mother. The egg was a "clone of the sheep that provided the DNA (and) sparked public concern about cloning humans."[109] For the first time, the miracle of creation had been changed. We no longer needed God's design.

God and Love

> *God loves each of us as if there were only one of us.*[110]
> —St. Augustine

The world defines love in two ways. It is a "strong affection for another arising out of kinship or personal ties (as maternal love for a child)" and an "attraction based on sexual desire; affection and tenderness felt by lovers."[111] Scripture tells us that Jesus defined it by saying,

> 'Love the Lord your God with all your heart and with all your soul and with all your mind and with all your strength.' The second is this: 'Love your neighbor as yourself.' There is no commandment greater than these.
>
> Mark 12:30–31 (NIV)

This is the heart of the problem, the duality of love. Looking at it another way, this gets to the heart of the problem. The problem is the duality of man.

The duality of man is simply the idea that "there are two equal powers—good and evil—in competition with one another...with equal power in competing with one another."[112] Nowhere is this idea more apparent than with love.

Because of the Fall, love has had to fight constantly, in the heart of every believer and nonbeliever. It has to fight every movie, every book, every social media site, every television site. Secularism has worked its way into everything. It has found its way into government buildings that display the Ten Commandments. It's in the messages given from many pulpits. Instead of God's love on display, it has to fight to even get mentioned.

Prayers to Use for Love

Most people have heard of the "Love Chapter." The verses are used a lot at weddings. In his letter to the church at Corinth, the Apostle Paul wrote,

> Love is patient, love is kind. It does not envy, it does not boast, it is not proud. It does not dishonor others, it is not self-seeking, it is not easily angered, it keeps no record of wrongs. Love does not delight in evil but rejoices with the truth. It always protects, always trusts, always hopes, always perseveres. Love never fails.
>
> 1 Corinthians 13:4–8 (NIV)

The key to love is to give all of yourself to someone else.

None of those, being patient, kind, humble, slow to anger, are easy to do. They also require you to treat others as equals. This is because to be patient or to be kind to someone, you must respect them. The opposite of these, being impatient, rude, boastful, and quick to anger, are the basis for many of the daily crimes committed.

God's Idea of Love

The reason God, in the form of Jesus, came to earth was because He loved us.

Over the course of his three-year ministry, he was betrayed by His Apostles because He carried the sins of the world on His shoulders; in days of His passion, He was separated from God. He was flogged with a cat-o-nine tail, mocked, spit on. He had his hands and feet nailed to a cross and crucified. What was His final wish as He was being crucified?

> And when they came to the place called The Skull, there they crucified Him and the criminals, one on the right and the other on the left. But Jesus was saying, 'Father, forgive them; for they do not know what they are doing.'
>
> Luke 23:33–34 (NASB)

He was asking forgiveness for the very people who were killing Him. That is a perfect example of agape love. Agape is "the most powerful, noblest type of love: sacrificial love. Agape love is more than a feeling—it is an act of the will."[113] Agape love is where you give unselfishly. Sex is the opposite as you are only concerned about giving to yourself.

Scripture tells us that "The word of God is alive and powerful. It is sharper than the sharpest two-edged sword, cutting between soul and spirit, between joint and marrow. It exposes our innermost thoughts and desires" (Hebrews 4:12, NLT). Therefore, since God is love, love is the most powerful thing we can use to fight the enemy with.

Man's Idea of Love

To understand a little about how sex seeped into every part of society, you must look at how ad writers how used sex to sell everything from soup to nuts.

It starts with the Gutenberg Press. Johannes Gensfleisch zur Laden zum Gutenberg was born in 1400 in the German city of Mainz, Rhine-Main area, the youngest son of the patrician merchant Friele Gensfleisch zur Laden, and his second wife, Else Wyrich. Little is known of his early life, although he would work as a goldsmith. Although the printing press itself was not new, he would make improvements to it.

By 1450, the press was in operation, thanks to Gutenberg for a loan of 800 guilders (equivalent to roughly 445 United States American Dollars). It not only revolutionized the printing industry but would help with the Great Commission. Hundreds of thousands of pages that would become known as the Gutenberg Bible would be printed. It was a *forty-two-line Bible*, printed on paper and some on vellum cardstock.

By the 19th century, newspapers in their current form did not exist, and with printing costs, even the largest only had a circulation of 300. All that changed in September 1833 when Benjamin Day created The Sun. Printed on small, letter-sized pages, *The Sun* sold for just a penny. The old printing press was capable of printing approximately 125 papers per hour; Day's idea increased this to approximately 18,000 copies per hour. He printed the paper's motto at the top of every front page of *The Sun*: "The object of this paper is to lay before the public, at a price within the means of everyone, all the news of the day, and at the same time offer an advantageous medium for advertisements."[114] Within two years, *The Sun* sold 15,000 copies per day. This idea would be copied by his competitors. That would be when the real problem began.

Advertisers began trying to compete for the same dollars and realized very quickly that sex sells. One of the earliest instances of this was the Pearl Tobacco Company. Since tobacco products were used by men, Pearl inserted, "In every cigarette package came trading cards featuring pictures of sexually appealing women."[115] Sales of the company's products doubled, then tripled. The skyrocketing sales made Pearl's competitors notice. Noticing how one simple idea had increased revenue, they followed suit with more pictures of naked women. This was followed by ads for other companies, with soap ads for both men and women. Sex sales and each company would now find ways to promote it.

With the gradual onslaught of sex in our daily lives, it would seem that sex would be the most important thing in our lives. Because of the insistent of this, many would start to believe it.

CHAPTER ELEVEN

The 2000s

Twenty hundred was a presidential election year for the United States. The candidates would both be the sons of prominent politicians.

The Republicans nominated George Walker Bush, the son of former president George Herbert Walker Bush. Bush senior had been on the national stage even before the presidency. He had been the leader of the Republican National Committee (RNC) and head of the Central Intelligence Agency (CIA) in the 1970s, and vice president under Ronald Reagan in the 1980s.

Bush the younger had a varied career before politics. After graduating from Harvard Business School in the mid-1970s, he began working in the oil industry. He also co-owned the Texas Rangers before becoming Texas governor in 1994. He would remain governor until his presidential nomination.

The Democrats nominated Albert Arnold Gore, Jr. Albert senior began his public service career in 1930. He would be Commissioner of the Tennessee Department of Labor and the United States Congress in the 1930s and would be serving in the United States Senate until 1970. Gore worked closely with President Johnson on several key issues in Johnson's Great Society program.

Gore junior attended Vanderbilt Law School in the 1970s before deciding to drop out and run for his dad's congressional seat, which he won. He would remain in the United States Congress until 1985 and then the United States Senate until he was elected vice president in 1992.

The election result, just as the one twenty years later, would be the focus of several weeks of news coverage. In 2000, the election came down to a few votes in Florida. On election night, news networks first called Florida for Gore later retracted the projection and then called Florida for Bush, before finally retracting that projection as well. Gore would first concede the election, then recant his concession. This would lead to a recount of Florida's votes.

The Florida recount was stopped a few weeks later by the US Supreme Court. They ruled the recount was unconstitutional and that no constitutionally valid recount could be completed by the December 12 deadline. This gave Bush the needed 271 electoral votes to Gore's 266. Two hundred seventy electoral votes are what is needed to become president. Gore would make history in one way, though. He would be the only presidential candidate who would be so untrusted by his home state that most of the voters would vote for his opponent.

The new millennium brings terrorism back to the forefront. On September 11, 2001, nineteen Islamic extremists hijacked four airplanes. American Airlines Flight 11 was flown into the north tower of the World Trade Center complex in Lower Manhattan at 8:46 a.m. United Airlines Flight 175 hit the south tower seventeen minutes later at 9:03 a.m. A third flight, American Airlines Flight 77, crashed into the Pentagon at 9:37 a.m. Finally, the fourth flight, United Airlines Flight 93, was flown toward Washington, DC. This plane crashed in a field near Shanksville, Pennsylvania, at 10:03 a.m., after passengers forced their way into the cockpit and fought the hijackers over the controls. Roughly 3000 Americans died because of the attacks. This would be the beginning of what President Bush deemed the War on Terror. American military began fighting Al Qaeda in Iraq and Afghanistan. The effects of the wars are still being felt in the United States and in parts of the world.

Just over one year later, another attack occurred, again, by Islamic extremists. On October 12, 2002, the tourist district of Kuta on the Indonesian island of Bali was attacked. The attack killed 202 people, and a further 240 people were injured. Terrorist attacks would become so common they would soon no longer rate a complete news cycle.

The explosion of the Internet ensured faster communication among people around the world. However, it also ensured that people would become more dependent on it. The first social networking sites, including Friendster, Myspace, Facebook, and Twitter, were established. Myspace was the most popular social networking website until June 2009, when Facebook overtook it.

One of the biggest reasons people would become "technological zombies" and stare at their phones for hours would hit the market during this decade. Apple would introduce the first iPhone, which combined three products "a revolutionary mobile phone, a widescreen iPod® with touch controls, and a breakthrough Internet communications device with desktop-class email, web browsing, searching and maps—into one small and lightweight handheld device."[116] This would help ensure that by the next decade, we would become slaves to technology.

Building upon Dolly the cloned sheep, mankind took the next step in convincing itself it did not need God. It was called the Human Genome Project (HGP), and it "gave us the ability, for the first time, to read nature's complete genetic blueprint for building a human being."[117] We were becoming convinced that not only did we not need both man and woman to create life, but that we could genetically make them better than God.

There would also be a worldwide financial meltdown in this decade. Although other financial crises would occur before 1929, none other were referred to as "depressions." Before then, they were called "panics." Whereas the Great Depression would be brought on, in many ways, by the stock market, the one eighty years later would be because of the interlocking banking system. This was followed by the European debt crisis, which began in Greece in late 2009, and the 2008–2011 Icelandic financial crisis.

A few of the larger banks were given a bailout of roughly $182 billion. Much as the Depression earlier, "the crisis created a run on money."[118] Three days later, Treasury Secretary Henry Paulson and Fed Chair Ben Bernanke submitted a $700 billion bailout package to Congress. Their fast response helped stop the run, but Republicans blocked the bill for two weeks because they didn't want to bail out banks. They only approved the bill on October 1, 2008, after global stock markets almost collapsed.

In 2008, many in the United States celebrated the election of Barack Hussein Obama as the 44th president. One of the typical quotes was, "Barack Obama elected as the president of the United States of America showed the whole world that minorities can also rule the world. It empowered, not the blacks themselves, but the soul of the African-Americans and other minority ethnic groups."[119] This means people like Frederick Douglass are being ignored. Frederick Douglass (born Frederick Augustus Washington Bailey) was born in February 1817. By the time of his death in 1895, he would be an American social reformer, abolitionist, orator, writer, and statesman. Not only did he become the guest of President Lincoln, but Douglass would also become the first black to receive nominating votes to become president during the 1888 Republican National Convention.

This means people like Nelson Mandela are being ignored. Nelson Rolihlahla Mandela was born on July 18, 1918. He was a South African anti-apartheid revolutionary, statesman, and philanthropist. He became South Africa's first black head of state in 1994 as he was elected President of South Africa that year in the first fully representative democratic election.

This means people like Dr. Martin Luther King, Jr. are being ignored. Martin Luther King Jr. was born on January 15, 1929. King was an American Baptist minister and activist. He would become the most visible spokesman and leader in American civil rights and later became the first president of the Southern Christian Leadership Conference (SCLC).

There would be hundreds more that could be mentioned, but you get the idea.

What's different is that Obama would be a Muslim, and he would set about undermining the Christian underpinnings of the United States. During his eight years in office, he gave money to Iran "$400 million in cash—stacks and stacks of currency in several national denominations."[120] He also gave money to the Muslim Brotherhood "$3 billion dollars in American taxpayer money...one day after making a historic speech in calling for Israel to give up Jerusalem."[121] Neither of those two should have surprised the American people if they had been paying attention.

Obama would be a Manchurian candidate type. He had been groomed to undermine the United States in any way he could. Obama's mentor was domestic terrorist Bill Ayers. Ayers was the founder of the Weather Underground (WU). By 1975, the group took credit "for 25 bombings—including the US Capitol, the Pentagon, the California Attorney General's office, and a New York City police station."[122] The WU had begun as a splinter group of the Students for a Democratic Society (SDS), and their intention was to "disrupt the empire...to incapacitate it, to put pressure on the cracks."[123] Furthermore, once the group disbanded, their leader, Bill Ayers, vowed to "radicalize America by working within, rather than outside of, the nation's mainstream institutions. In particular, he sought to embed himself in a position of influence within the education establishment."[124] He would do this in 1987 by earning a doctorate from Columbia University's Teachers College and becoming a professor of education at the University of Illinois. The man who used to chant, "Kill all the rich people...Bring the revolution home. Kill your parents"[125] was now in a position of authority over young adults whose minds are easily influenced. By this time in his life, Ayers had surrendered to authorities and, due to a technicality, was never sentenced.

This should not have been the end of the story. However, there was no media coverage. More importantly, there was no media outrage. The man who was, by his own admission, "guilty as sin, free as a bird."[126] It would be similar to one of the leaders of the Ku Klux Klan becoming President. Candidate Obama would say in one of his last campaign speeches: "We are five days away from fundamentally transforming the United States of America...we will change this country and we will change the world."[127] These were the truest words the former president would ever speak.

God and Stewardship

> *We must strive to become good ancestors.*[128]
> —Ralph Nader

Both of the candidates running for the United States President in 2000 would have a huge impact on the coming decade. One, George W. Bush, would become president. The other would begin to wage a campaign against global warming. Whether you believe man is powerful enough to change the temperature of the earth depends on essentially how you vote. That's because manmade global warming has become just another easy soundbite, no different than gun rights or abortion. This has happened in large part because of Gore.

Gore would make a documentary in 2006 in which he would claim that "Global warming, along with the cutting and burning of forests and other critical habitats, is causing the loss of living species at a level comparable to the extinction event that wiped out the dinosaurs 65 million years ago. That event was believed to have been caused by a giant asteroid. This time it is not an asteroid colliding with the Earth and wreaking havoc: it is us."[129] However, the documentary was "found by a British judge to contain nine errors. The judge said it could not be shown to students unless it included a notice pointing out the errors."[130] Instead of correcting, Gore doubled down with lectures, books, and another documentary. As of this writing, Gore's net worth is roughly $30 billion. Not bad for someone who was a public servant for forty years.

Prayers for Stewardship

We know that "every faculty you have, your power of thinking or of moving your limbs from moment to moment, is given you by God. If you devoted every moment of your whole life exclusively to His service, you could not give Him anything that was not in a sense His own already."[131] Everything, *everything*, we own is not really ours. Just as in the Garden of Eden, we are caretakers for the things that He owns.

The number of things we care for has changed since the Fall, but one thing hasn't. We have to do all we can to protect the earth. The problem comes, though, from the term "manmade global warming." We have convinced ourselves that we either "destroy" the earth or "save" the earth. Actually, we are just custodians.

God's Idea of Stewardship

King David tells us that "The earth is the LORD's, and everything in it, the world, and all who live in it" (Psalm 24:1, NIV). It would be David who would begin life as a simple sheepherder and would become one of the greatest kings in history. However, as much power as he had, he prayed,

> Yours, LORD, is the greatness, the power, the glory, the victory, and the majesty, indeed everything that is in the heavens and on the earth; Yours is the dominion, LORD, and You exalt Yourself as head over all. Both riches

and honor come from You, and You rule over all, and in Your hand is power and might; and it lies in Your hand to make great and to strengthen everyone. Now therefore, our God, we thank You, and praise Your glorious name. But who am I and who are my people that we should be able to offer as generously as this? For all things come from You, and from Your hand we have given to You. For we are strangers before You, and temporary residents, as all our fathers were; our days on the earth are like a shadow, and there is no hope.

1 Chronicles 29:11–15 (NASB)

King David had a heart for God because David always remembered he was a shepherd.

Man's Idea of Stewardship

Hundreds upon hundreds of individuals have become converts of the religion of global warming. One of the earliest in the United States was Gaylord Nelson. Nelson was born on June 4, 1916, in Clear Lake, Wisconsin. Like many before and after him, he used his time in the military as a catapult for elected office.

In 1948, Nelson was elected to the Wisconsin State Senate. He would hold public office, either as governor or United States senator, until 1980. In the late 1960s, he would push legislation through that would create Earth Day, which began as a "teach-in" on April 22, 1970. On that day, "20 million Americans—at the time, 10 percent of the total population of the United States—took to the streets, parks, and auditoriums to demonstrate against the impacts of 150 years of industrial development which had left a growing legacy of serious human health impacts."[132] Nelson would use his time in office to push for environmental issues and was totally unconcerned about economic ones. Earth Day would be, in many ways, the father of the environmentalist movement. A movement that would, over the next fifty years, look more like the one Nelson envisioned where environmental issues would become important than economic ones.

CHAPTER TWELVE

The 2010s

The definition of truth does not change. It has not changed since "The Beginning." The problem is that as much of the world today runs counter to God's teaching, the world has tried to redefine truth.

If it is not true, it is a lie. Even children know that. The problem is that even believers use the term "your truth." The problem is not there is not your truth, or my truth, simply *the* truth. Many of us do not like a lot of what is in Scripture. There is murder, rape, incest, and every other sin imaginable. Many churches today only preach about "safe" topics. Much of the Book of Romans isn't discussed because it condemns homosexuality.

Many don't preach from the Pentateuch, as it not only defines the Fall (which means man is not in control) but gives much of the history of God's people and His commandments. Believers should want to know their history and the commandments. But again, a lot of modern believers, pastors included, have very weak faith. The stories such as the parting of the red sea and the flood would be unbelievable to many. As for the commandments, many of them (thou shalt not steal, thou shalt not commit adultery) hit too close to home.

God and Truth

In a time of universal deceit—telling the truth is a revolutionary act.[133]

—George Orwell

We've all heard people say today, "That's your truth, but that's not my truth." Second United States President John Adams said, "Our Constitution was made only for a moral and religious people. It is wholly inadequate to the government of any other."[134] There are many who say that America was never a Christian nation. However, further examination says otherwise. But, let's start at the beginning.

In 1620, the Pilgrims left their comfortable homes in England and sailed for the new country for religious freedom. One hundred and two men, women, and children undertook a dangerous journey in a boat called the Mayflower, not knowing if or when they would survive.

Upon their arrival, they thanked God, then they created what has since been termed the Mayflower Compact. The Compact said that they had "undertaken for the Glory of God, and Advancement of the Christian

Faith, and the Honour of our King and Country, a Voyage to plant the first Colony in the northern Parts of *Virginia*; Do by these Presents, solemnly and mutually...covenant and combine ourselves together into a civil Body Politick, for our better Ordering and Preservation, and Furtherance of the Ends aforesaid: And by Virtue hereof do enact, constitute, and frame, such just and equal Laws, Ordinances, Acts, Constitutions, and Officers, from time to time, as shall be thought most meet and convenient for the general Good of the Colony; unto which we promise all due Submission and Obedience."[135] The compact was then used in part on the House of Burgesses.

In 1619, the English Monarch King James sent George Yeardley to the colonies to establish a government in Virginia. Upon his arrival, Yeardley, now Governor, stated he was going to "abolish martial law and create a legislative assembly, known as the General Assembly—the first legislative assembly in the American colonies."[136] In 1643, the General Assembly became a bicameral body and would begin to include the descendants of the Pilgrims. Famous elected members of the House of Burgess included George Washington and Thomas Jefferson.

At the time that the United States of America was founded in 1776, no country had attempted to govern itself. America was not founded as a "democracy," although many have been miseducated to believe that it was. While they are similar, the difference is that in a republic, "laws are made by representatives chosen by the people and must comply with a constitution that specifically protects the rights of the minority from the will of the majority."[137] Whereas in a democracy, the minority has no voice.

Many of America's founders, Thomas Jefferson, for example, were in no way believers. Jefferson would go so far as have his own version of the Bible, in which he cut out every miracle Jesus performed. He was enough of a realist, however, to admit that if the new nation did not include a system of government based on the compact, it would fail.

The United States would not only succeed but thrive. This is due, in large part, because of the Christian beliefs that are interwoven into the Declaration of Independence. The Declaration declared that "we hold these truths to be self-evident, that all men are created equal, that they are endowed by their Creator with certain unalienable Rights, that among these are Life, Liberty and the pursuit of Happiness."[138] By stating in such a straightforward manner that the United States would either fall or flourish thanks to their belief. Nations and foreign people alike took notice when America became a superpower in just over one hundred years.

That's why dozens of countries in the 20th century became Representative Republics. Today, a search will reveal that more and more countries are following suit. Not because America's Founding Fathers were great men, but because they believed that following Christ was the only way to run a life, a family, or a country.

The farthest away from God's teachings America moves, the more John Adams is proven right.

Prayers for Truth

There is a reason the idea of "truth" is taken so seriously. During a trial, an oath is sworn to the effect of: "Do you solemnly swear to tell the truth, the whole truth and nothing but the truth?"[139] During that same trial, after people are caught lying while under oath, they will be punished up to and including going to jail. Likewise, the idea of being truthful or suffering the results of lying can be seen throughout history. Truth is not a secular invention. Philosophers speak about truth; children play the game Truth or Dare. Parents punish their children when they find out they're lying. There was a popular game show for two decades called *Truth or Consequences*.

The idea of living and speaking the truth or else is enforced by Scripture. The Apostle John writes, "Then you will know the truth, and the truth will set you free"

(John 8:32, NIV). Therefore, it is not only the duty of believers to continually search for truth; it is our obligation to point nonbelievers to it as well.

God's Idea of Truth

In the Book of John, we read, "Jesus said to him, 'I am the way, the truth, and the life. No one comes to the Father except through Me'" (John 14:6, NKJV). Therefore, it is our responsibility as believers to direct others to the truth. So if Jesus is "the truth," we are to direct others to Him. We must also remember that "Jesus Christ the same yesterday, and to day, and for ever" (Hebrews 13:8, KJV). That must also mean that the truth does not change.

Man's Idea of Truth

Instead, we have become a world where we hear the phrase, "This is my truth." What does this mean? There are organizations, Black Lives Matter (BLM) and Antifa, to name just two, who have created agendas to transform, or more correctly, to undermine, the Christian civilizations.

BLM believes that "black liberation movements in this country have created room, space, and leadership mostly for black heterosexual, cisgender men—leaving women, queer and transgender people, and others either out of the movement or in the background to move the work forward."[140] Sadly, many churches have accepted the lie that the truth can change.

Churches today, regardless of denomination, have chosen to embrace this lie by cloaking it in the ideas of "diversity" and "inclusion." One typical example of this is one church's website that "welcomes people of every race, gender, gender identity, sexual orientation, marital status, age, physical and mental ability, national origin, economic station, and political ideology (with)... all members, without exception, being fully eligible to participate in the ordinances, blessings, benefits and responsibilities of church membership—including communion, baptism, marriage, ordination, parent/child dedications, and all offices and positions of leadership."[141] This was taken from the website of a First Baptist Church (FBC). Most FBCs are members of the Southern Baptist Convention, a conservatively minded association. However, churches are leaving the SBC and becoming more liberal in thought. The reason, of course, is money.

People today are chasing "easy." If something makes us "uncomfortable" or is "too hard," we walk away. Our world is littered with broken relationships. Marriages are walked away from, families are torn apart, friendships are forgotten, and church membership declines.

Why? Because someone said something that shined a little truth. So instead of being willing to stand in the light of truth and honestly look at ourselves, we have chosen to redefine truth to whatever we want it to be at that moment.

One of the phrases made popular in the 1960s is "If it feels good, do it." The idea of "That's your truth; this is my truth" is the logical extension of that. The problem, however, is that we as believers are called to be:

> The salt of the earth. But if the salt loses its saltiness, how can it be made salty again? It is no longer good for anything, except to be thrown out and trampled underfoot. You are the light of the world. A town built on a hill cannot be hidden. Neither do people light a lamp and put it under a bowl. Instead, they put it on its stand, and it gives light to everyone in the house.
>
> Matthew 5:13–15 (NIV)

How can we use the fallen world as our spiritual north?

This can be seen in churches amending their bylaws in order to be more "inclusive." The national organizations instruct the local churches to "consider adding language to sections on mission, membership, and employment, and/or adding a section that addresses affirmation and promotion in all activities and endeavors, including membership, programming, hiring practices, and the calling of religious professionals. Consider how to incorporate both nondiscrimination language and affirmation or inclusion language."[142] It has become more important to offend God than to offend man.

CHAPTER THIRTEEN

The 2020s

By the beginning of the century's second decade, less than 50 percent of Americans were church members. Compare this to when it was first measured, the 1930s. At that time, it was 73 percent and "remained near 70 percent for the next six decades, before beginning a steady decline around the turn of the 21st century."[143] This is only the number of church members; the number of regular attendees has steadily decreased since the 1950s.

God and Togetherness

We must learn to live together as brothers or perish together as fools.[144]

—Martin Luther King, Jr.

Another word that has had its definition changed is "together." At the end of 2019, the world was hit with a pandemic. Regardless of which side of the political aisle you find yourself on, you can't argue that the pandemic was used for political purposes. One of the phrases used during this time was: "We're all in this together," and one of the organizations that used it politically was the United Nations (UN). In April 2020, only months after a worldwide call to shut businesses down, stay home, and "flatten the curve," the UN had a different idea. They were using COVID-19 as a way to push "human rights." "The message is clear: People—and their rights—must be front and centre. A human rights lens puts everyone in the picture and ensures that no one is left behind. Human rights responses can help beat the pandemic, putting a focus on the imperative of healthcare for everyone."[145] I'm sure it's comforting for all of those who lost loved ones during the pandemic that millions of dollars have been used to push an agenda.

Prayers for Togetherness

We have an idea of togetherness from the Book of Revelation. The Apostle John writes,

> Then I heard every creature in heaven and on earth and under the earth and on the sea, and all that is in them, saying: 'To him who sits on the throne and to the Lamb be praise and honor and glory and power, for ever and ever!'
>
> Revelation 5:13 (NIV)

Imagine that! That is togetherness.

The world creates an endless supply of pettiness based on politics, day-to-day difficulties, and other trivialities. These were created by Satan eons ago to divide us. They have worked exceedingly well. Despite calls for unity, we are more divided now than at any other point in history. We should pray to be able to ignore the pettiness. When that occurs, we can begin to see togetherness as God intended.

God's Idea of Togetherness

There are many examples of togetherness. However, one of the last things Jesus showed us during His time on earth. He would pray, "That all of them may be one, Father, just as you are in me and I am in you. May they also be in us so that the world may believe that you have sent me" (John 17:21, NIV). Jesus was praying that believers would be as close to each other as He was to the Father. That is togetherness!

Man's Idea of Togetherness

It's been talked about earlier, but the COVID-19 pandemic was used as a power grab by multiple world leaders. It was done under the guise of togetherness, as in we're all in this together. "We are all in this together. The virus threatens everyone. Human rights uplift everyone. By respecting human rights in this time of crisis, we will build more effective and inclusive solutions for the emergency of today and the recovery for tomorrow."[146] Instead of trying to truthfully deal with the outbreak, most countries chose instead to try to terrify their citizens. What was the only solution they gave? To look to them for every answer.

Togetherness is never putting one over the other. It is never about misusing any information. It is never about much of what happened during the various lockdowns. Satan used the pandemic to shut down schools, businesses, and, most importantly, churches. Family get-togethers were canceled. There were worldwide shortages of everything from food to toilet paper. The problem was that very few complained.

In a world where there are over 2 billion Christians, there was very little push back. The problem is that we believe that elected leaders have our best interests at heart. Even when there are centuries of history that say otherwise. The Apostle Paul says,

> Let everyone be subject to the governing authorities, for there is no authority except that which God has established. The authorities that exist have been established by God. Consequently, whoever rebels against the author-

ity is rebelling against what God has instituted, and those who do so will bring judgment on themselves.

Romans 13:1–2 (NIV)

Millions of believers believe this means we should blindly follow our elected leaders. If that is true, does that mean that God is okay with leaders who push abortion? Does He want His followers to vote for and support leaders who are anti-Israel? Are we supposed to be okay with everything our leaders do?

No. Earthly leaders are like us, sinful. He wants us to be discerning about which ones to vote for, support, and follow. Unless we as believers do that, we will be no better, or worse, than nonbelievers.

Epilogue

There is no neutral ground in the universe. Every square inch, every split second is claimed by God and counterclaimed by Satan.[147]

—C. S. Lewis

The book ends the way it began, with a quote from C. S. Lewis. That was done to reinforce how important that view is.

Satan, the enemy of all believers, to use a sports analogy has what is called a "long game." That long game started in the Garden of Eden when he spoke his first lie to Eve. He has continued to work his way into every life, every home, and every church since then. There have been moments in our history where he has made major inroads. However, since 1900, the church, small "c," has allowed itself to listen to all those voices that Satan used.

For example, there are organizations, Black Lives Matter (BLM) and Antifa, to name just two, who have created agendas to transform, or more correctly, to undermine, the Christian civilizations.

Where once believers faith was strong, Communism and Socialism have worked their way in. Since the core belief of these two is the power of man, these two ideas cannot coexist.

Law and order are being undermined. These are laws that were drawn up based on God's laws.

We've gone from God bless you to wishing everyone "Good Vibes."

But since 1900, the Church, big "C," has not changed.

God is still on the throne.

He is still faithful. He still answers prayers.

What has changed?

We have.

Those of us who swore before the Creator to be as faithful to Him as He is to us.

Those of us who have forgotten that first fire of conversion.

Those of us who have accepted comfort. Those of us who have accepted the church that is being passed on to those who don't know differently.

The time is not too late. There are things we can do. Start a Bible study in our home. Minister to others. Do not accept mediocrity.

He is watching.

Endnotes

1. C. S. Lewis quote. Retrieved from https://www.goodreads.com/quotes/755193-there-is-no-neutral-ground-in-the-universe-every-square
2. C. S. Lewis quote. Retrieved from https://www.azquotes.com/quote/462403
3. America's Changing Religious Landscape. Pew Research. Retrieved from https://www.pewforum.org/2015/05/12/americas-changing-religious-landscape/
4. YMCA. Retrieved from https://www.ymca.int/george-williams/
5. Salvation Army. History. Retrieved from https://story.salvationarmy.org/
6. History of Motion Pictures. Retrieved from https://www.pbs.org/wgbh/americanexperience/features/pickford-early-history-motion-pictures/
7. Henry Adams. Retrieved from https://invention.si.edu/1900-world-s-fair-produced-dazzling-dynamos-great-art-and-our-current-conversation-about-technology
8. Henry Adams quote. Retrieved from https://www.azquotes.com/author/84-Henry_Adams
9. William McKinley. *Decision on the Philippines.* Re-

trieved from https://www.digitalhistory.uh.edu/disp_textbook.cfm?smtID=3&psid=1257
10 Helen Keller quote. Retrieved from https://www.quotes.net/quote/51977
11 Industrial Revolution. Retrieved from https://www.history.com/topics/industrial-revolution/industrial-revolution
12 History of the Sewing Machine. Retrieved from https://www.thoughtco.com/stitches-the-history-of-sewing-machines-1992460
13 Revenue Act of 1861. Retrieved from http://self.gutenberg.org/articles/Revenue_Act_of_1861
14 Rockefeller quotes. Retrieved from https://quotes.thefamouspeople.com/john-d-rockefeller-172.php
15 Rockefeller Philanthropy. Retrieved from https://faithandpubliclife.com/the-men-who-built-america-john-d-rockefeller-s-faith/#http://valuesandcapitalism.com/dialogue/society/men-who-built-america
16 Retrieved from https://iww.org/membership/
17 Unemployment and Health Insurance in Great Britain, 1911-37. Retrieved from https://www.ssa.gov/policy/docs/ssb/v1n8/v1n8p23.pdf
18 Scouting for Boys 1907. Retrieved from https://bpsa-us.org/pdf/yarns00-281.pdf
19 Boy Scouts. Retrieved from https://www.scouting.org/about/
20 Titanic quote. Retrieved from https://www.archives.gov/exhibits/american_originals/titanic.html
21 Henry Clay and the Law. Retrieved from https://www.lehrmaninstitute.org/history/Andrew-Jackson-1837.html#rechartering
22 Jackson Specie Circular. Retrieved from Jackson Specie Circular. Retrieved from https://www.sjsu.edu/faculty/watkins/speciescircular.htm

23 Patrick Henry quote. Retrieved from http://liberty-tree.ca/quotes/Patrick.Henry.Quote.7125
24 Edward Gibbon, *The Decline and Fall of the Roman Empire*, 32. Retrieved from https://freeclassicebooks.com/Edward%20Gibbon/The%20History%20of%20The%20Decline%20and%20Fall%20of%20the%20Roman%20Empire%20Vol%202.pdf
25 *Britannica Online*. "Acts of Uniformity." Retrieved from https://www.britannica.com/topic/Acts-of-Uniformity
26 Martin Luther King, *95 Theses*. Retrieved from https://www.luther.de/en/95thesen.html
27 J. R. Wilson sermon. Retrieved from https://www.civilwarcauses.org/revwilson.htm
28 Address in Pueblo, Colorado. Retrieved from https://www.presidency.ucsb.edu/documents/address-the-city-hall-auditorium-pueblo-colorado
29 Ibid.
30 Retrieved from https://www.marxists.org/archive/lenin/works/1913/nov/00mg.htm
31 Herbert Hoover quote. Retrieved from https://americainclass.org/sources/becomingmodern/prosperity/text1/text1.htm
32 Eighteenth Amendment. Retrieved from https://constitution.congress.gov/constitution/amendment-18/
33 1920s Revival. Retrieved from http://www.evanwiggs.com/revival/history/3-1900.html
34 Bruce Barton, *The Man Nobody Knows*. Retrieved from https://americainclass.org/sources/becomingmodern/prosperity/text2/mannobodyknows.pdf
35 Money quote. Retrieved from https://www.brainyquote.com/quotes/henry_fielding_195350
36 *Merriam Webster Online*. "Barter." Retrieved from https://www.merriam-webster.com/dictionary/barter

37 *Money and Man.* The Mises Institute. Retrieved from https://mises.org/library/money-and-man
38 *Britannica Online.* "Keynesian Economics." Retrieved from https://www.britannica.com/topic/Keynesian-economics
39 Joseph Goebbels quote. Retrieved from https://www.inspiringquotes.us/quotes/TzEs_7CxEctuv
40 Quadragesimo Anno. Retrieved from http://pdf.amazingdiscoveries.org/References/RtR/PDF-903/Pius%20XI,%20Quadragesimo%20Anno.pdf
41 Chuck Colson Speaks. Promise Press, 2000, 53.
42 *Merriam Webster Online.* "Family." Retrieved from https://www.merriam-webster.com/dictionary/family
43 Washington Farewell Address. Retrieved from https://thefederalistpapers.org/wp-content/uploads/2012/12/Washingtons-Farewell-Address-.pdf
44 Cicero quote. Referred from https://www.goodreads.com/quotes/49233-in-times-of-war-the-law-falls-silent-silent-enim
45 *Merriam Webster Online.* "Cubit." Retrieved from https://www.merriam-webster.com/dictionary/cubit
46 *Merriam Webster Online.* "Span." Retrieved from https://www.merriam-webster.com/dictionary/span
47 How A Day of Prayer Saved Britain. Referenced from https://www.premierchristianity.com/Blog/How-a-day-of-prayer-saved-Britain-at-Dunkirk
48 *Merriam Webster Online.* "No Quarter." Retrieved from https://www.merriam-webster.com/dictionary/no%20quarter
49 *Merriam Webster Online.* "Arianism." Retrieved from https://www.britannica.com/topic/Arianism
50 Battle of Tolbiac. Referenced from http://self.gutenberg.org/articles/Battle_of_Tolbiac

51 The Art of War. Retrieved from https://www.utoledo.edu › rotc › pdfs › the_art_of_war.pdf
52 History. Neville Chamberlain. Retrieved from https://www.history.com/news/chamberlain-declares-peace-for-our-time-75-years-ago
53 United Nations. Charter. Retrieved from https://www.un.org/en/about-us/un-charter/chapter-1
54 1950s Workplace. Retrieved from https://www.khanacademy.org/humanities/us-history/postwarera/1950s-america/a/women-in-the-1950s
55 "A History of the Date." Retrieved from https://ushist2112honors.files.wordpress.com/2010/08/bailey-courtship.pdf
56 Edmund Burke quote. Retrieved from http://www.thetimewall.com/edmund-burke-1729-1797-those-who-dont-know-history-are-destined-to-repeat-it-george-santayana-1863-1952-those-who-cannot-remember-the-past-are-condemned-to-repeat-it/
57 Buchanan County History. Retrieved from https://www.buchanancountyhistory.com/oneroomschool.php
58 New England Primer. Retrieved from https://digital.library.pitt.edu/islandora/object/pitt%3A00acj3379m/viewer#page/116/mode/2up
59 Massachusetts.gov. Retrieved from https://www.mass.gov/files/documents/2016/08/ob/deludersatan.pdf
60 History. Magna Carta. Retrieved from https://d1lexza0zk46za.cloudfront.net/history/am-docs/magna-carta.pdf
61 The Federalist Papers. Retrieved from https://www.thefederalistpapers.org/wp-content/uploads/2012/12/The-Mayflower-Compact1.pdf
62 *Eisenhower Library Online.* "Religion." Retrieved

from https://www.eisenhowerlibrary.gov/eisenhowers/quotes#Religion
63 Society for Promoting Christian Knowledge Schools. Retrieved from https://spckpublishing.co.uk/spck-history
64 National Secular Society. Retrieved from https://www.secularism.org.uk/what-is-secularism.html
65 Communist Reign of Terror Killed 200,000 Clergymen Retrieved from http://www.paulbogdanor.com/left/soviet/atheism2.html
66 Retrieved from https://journals.plos.org/plosone/article?id=10.1371/journal.pone.0121454
67 Religious Education. Retrieved from https://www.gov.uk/national-curriculum/other-compulsory-subjects
68 Buddhism. Retrieved from https://thebuddhistcentre.com/buddhism
69 Divorce Rate 1960s. Retrieved from https://www.virginialeenlaw.com/help/what-was-the-divorce-rate-in-1960.html
70 The Second Sex. Retrieved from https://www.the-philosophy.com/de-beauvoir-born-woman
71 Ibid.
72 "The Feminine Mystique." Retrieved from https://nationalhumanitiescenter.org/ows/seminars/tcentury/FeminineMystique.pdf
73 Pauli Murray. Retrieved from https://now.org/about/history/finding-pauli-murray/
74 Tolkien quote. Retrieved from https://www.goodreads.com/quotes/471515-many-that-live-deserve-death-and-some-that-die-deserve
75 *Dictionary Online*. "Truth." Retrieved from https://www.dictionary.com/browse/truth
76 *Cambridge Dictionary Online*. "Right." Retrieved

from https://dictionary.cambridge.org/dictionary/english/right
77 *Dictionary Online.* "Justice." Retrieved from https://www.dictionary.com/browse/justice
78 Mayflower Compact. Retrieved from https://www.mayflowercompact.org/
79 Declaration of Independence. Retrieved from https://www.archives.gov/founding-docs/declaration-transcript
80 European Union In Brief. Retrieved from https://europa.eu/european-union/about-eu/eu-in-brief_en
81 Ibid.
82 Black Panther Party Ten Points. Retrieved from https://www.collectiveliberation.org/wp-content/uploads/2015/01/BPP_Ten_Point_Program.pdf
83 Roe V. Wade. Retrieved from https://supreme.findlaw.com/supreme-court-insights/roe-v--wade-case-summary--what-you-need-to-know.html
84 Earth Day History. Retrieved from https://www.earthday.org/history/
85 Earth Day Successes. Retrieved from https://www.earthday.org/our-successes/
86 Ford's Military Service. Retrieved from https://www.fordlibrarymuseum.gov/grf/naval.htm
87 Ford's First Press Conference. Retrieved from https://archive.org/details/CSPAN3_20140811_044500_President_Fords_First_News_Conference
88 President Ford and Evangelical Leaders. Retrieved from https://www.fordlibrarymuseum.gov/library/document/0204/1511927.pdf
89 Mother Theresa quotes. Retrieved from https://www.rd.com/list/forgiveness-quotes/
90 CNN lead story. Retrieved from https://www.history.com/this-day-in-history/cnn-launches

91 Invention of Computers. Retrieved from https://www.rediscoverthe80s.com/2020/05/major-world-events-of-1980s.html
92 Pope John Paul. Retrieved from https://www.pbs.org/wgbh/pages/frontline/shows/pope/etc/faith.html
93 Reagan Commencement Speech. Retrieved from https://www.presidency.ucsb.edu/documents/address-commencement-exercises-eureka-college-illinois
94 Reagan and God quote. Retrieved from https://familycouncil.org/?p=8656
95 Margaret Thatcher on Socialism. Retrieved from https://fee.org/articles/margaret-thatcher-on-socialism-20-of-her-best-quotes/
96 Tony Blair. Retrieved from https://www.eternitynews.com.au/archive/margaret-thatcher-on-god-and-politics/
97 Margaret Thatcher and God. Retrieved from https://www.eternitynews.com.au/archive/margaret-thatcher-on-god-and-politics/
98 Gallup. Retrieved from https://news.gallup.com/poll/341963/church-membership-falls-below-majority-first-time.aspx
99 Church Stats. Retrieved from https://www.christian-research.org/reports/archives-and-statistics/uk-church-overview/
100 John Bunyan quote. Retrieved from https://www.goodreads.com/quotes/401457-prayer-will-make-a-man-cease-from-sin-or-sin
101 *Merriam Webster Online.* "Legalism." Retrieved from https://www.merriam-webster.com/dictionary/legalism
102 Mayflower History. Retrieved from http://mayflowerhistory.com/religion

103 Lewinsky Remarks. Retrieved from https://www.presidency.ucsb.edu/documents/remarks-the-after-school-child-care-initiative

104 Bill Clinton and the Meaning of Is. Retrieved from https://slate.com/news-and-politics/1998/09/bill-clinton-and-the-meaning-of-is.html

105 Music Ratings. Retrieved from https://www.newsweek.com/2015/10/09/oral-history-tipper-gores-war-explicit-rock-lyrics-dee-snider-373103.html

106 Reagan Speech "Tear Down This Wall." Retrieved from https://www.presidency.ucsb.edu/documents/remarks-east-west-relations-the-brandenburg-gate-west-berlin

107 Megachurches. Retrieved from https://www.astudyofdenominations.com/movements/mega-church/

108 Church Attendance in the 1990's. Retrieved from https://churchleaders.com/pastors/pastor-articles/139575-7-startling-facts-an-up-close-look-at-church-attendance-in-america.html/2

109 Dolly the Sheep. Retrieved from https://www.abc.net.au/science/features/biotech/1990.htm

110 St. Augustine Quote. Retrieved from https://www.brainyquote.com/authors/saint-augustine-quotes

111 *Merriam Webster Online*. "Love." Retrieved from https://www.merriam-webster.com/dictionary/love

112 Duality of man. Retrieved from https://www.compellingtruth.org/dualism.html

113 Agape Love. Retrieved from https://www.gotquestions.org/phileo-love.html

114 The Penny Press. Retrieved from https://awealthofcommonsense.com/2020/02/a-short-history-of-advertising/

115 Pearl Advertising. Retrieved from https://mbenisz.

wordpress.com/history-of-sex-in-advertising/
116 iPhone. Retrieved from https://www.apple.com/newsroom/2007/01/09Apple-Reinvents-the-Phone-with-iPhone/
117 Human Genome. Retrieved from https://www.genome.gov/human-genome-project
118 2008 Financial Crisis. Retrieved from https://www.thebalance.com/2008-financial-crisis-3305679
119 Barack Obama Election quote. Retrieved from https://www.thetoptens.com/important-events-2000s/
120 Obama-Iran deal. Retrieved from https://www.washingtontimes.com/news/2016/aug/18/iran-ransom-humiliates-obama/
121 Obama-Muslim Brotherhood. Retrieved from https://www.judiciaryreport.com/why_has_obama_given_billions_of_dollars_to_a_terrorist_organization.htm
122 Federal Bureau of Investigation. Weather Underground Bombings. Retrieved fromhttps://www.fbi.gov/history/famous-cases/weather-underground-bombings
123 Ibid.
124 Discover The Networks. Bill Ayers. Retrieved from https://www.discoverthenetworks.org/individuals/bill-ayers/
125 Ibid.
126 Jay Nordlinger, "Guilty as Sin, Free as a Bird," 2008. Retrieved from https://www.nationalreview.com/corner/guilty-sin-free-bird-jay-nordlinger/
127 Barack Obama Fundamentally Transforming Quote. Retrieved from https://www.presidency.ucsb.edu/documents/remarks-columbia-missouri-0
128 Ralph Nader quote. Retrieved from https://www.

brainyquote.com/quotes/ralph_nader_454614

129 Al Gore quote. Retrieved from https://www.goodreads.com/author/quotes/5658.Al_Gore

130 Problems with Gore movie. Retrieved from https://www.investors.com/politics/editorials/al-gore-runs-global-warming-racket/

131 *Mere Christianity.* C. S. Lewis. McMillian Publishing 1943. Page 92.

132 Earth Day History. Retrieved from https://www.earthday.org/history/

133 George Orwell quote. Retrieved from https://www.goodreads.com/quotes/451258-during-times-of-universal-deceit-telling-the-truth-becomes-a

134 John Adams quote. Retrieved from https://www.azquotes.com/author/90-John_Adams

135 ayflower Compact. Retrieved from https://www.mayflowercompact.org/

136 House of Burgess. Retrieved from https://www.ushistory.org/us/2f.asp

137 Representative Republic. Retrieved from https://www.thoughtco.com/republic-vs-democracy-4169936

138 Declaration of Independence. Retrieved from https://www.archives.gov/founding-docs/declaration-transcript

139 To Tell the Truth Oath. Retrieved from https://converus.com/blog/tell-the-truth/

140 Black Lives Matter. History. Retrieved from https://blacklivesmatter.com/herstory/

141 First Baptist Church of Washington, DC. Statement of Inclusion. Retrieved from https://www.firstbaptistdc.org/statement-of-inclusion

142 United Unitarianism Association. Retrieved from https://www.uua.org/lgbtq/welcoming/ways/wel-

come-statements

143 Church Attendance. Retrieved from https://news.gallup.com/poll/341963/church-membership-falls-below-majority-first-time.aspx

144 Martin Luther King, Jr. Quote. Retrieved from https://www.brainyquote.com/quotes/martin_luther_king_jr_101309

145 We're All In This Together. The United Nations. Retrieved from https://www.un.org/en/un-coronavirus-communications-team/we-are-all-together-human-rights-and-covid-19-response-and

146 We're All In This Together. Retrieved from https://www.un.org/en/un-coronavirus-communications-team/we-are-all-together-human-rights-and-covid-19-response-and

147 C. S. Lewis quote. Retrieved from https://www.goodreads.com/quotes/755193-there-is-no-neutral-ground-in-the-universe-every-square